SPECTRUM MICRO DRIVE BOOK

with details of the **ZX Interface 1**;
the **Microdrive**, the **Local Area Network**
and the **RS232 Link**

by Dr. Ian Logan

MELBOURNE HOUSE

Published in the United Kingdom by:
Melbourne House (Publishers) Ltd.,
Melbourne House,
Church Yard,
Tring, Hertfordshire HP23 5LU,
ISBN 0 - 86161 - 127 - 6

Published in Australia by:
Melbourne House (Australia) Pty. Ltd.,
Suite 4, 75 Palmerston Crescent,
South Melbourne, Victoria, 3205,
National Library of Australia Card Number and
ISBN 0 - 86759 - 128 - 5

Published in the United States of America by:
Melbourne House Software Inc.,
347 Reedwood Drive,
Nashville TN 37217.

Copyright (c) 1983 Dr I. Logan

All rights reserved. This book is copyright. No part of this book may be copied or stored by any means whatsoever whether mechanical or electronic, except for private or study use as defined in the Copyright Act. All enquiries should be addressed to the publishers

Printed in Hong Kong by Colorcraft Ltd.
1st Edition

Preface:

The long awaited **Microdrives** have now appeared. They allow owners of the **ZX Spectrum** to save and retrieve their programs and data using a sophisticated mass storage device. But, not only have the **Microdrives** arrived — there are also the **Local Area Network** and the **RS232** Link.

Each **Microdrive** and **ZX Interface 1** is supplied with a manual that introduces the user to the new **Spectrum** system; but in such a 'beginner's manual' there are many questions left unanswered. In this book there are chapters on the extended **Spectrum** system, the extended BASIC, the **Microdrive**, the **Local Area Network**, the **RS232** link and finally the information required by the machine code programmer.

The aim of the book is really one of trying to answer the questions that will be posed by owners of the new equipment; and the book does not try to list programs that can be written to use the new features.

It has only been possible for me to envisage the writing of this book because I have had the pleasure of assisting in the writing of the 'shadow' ROM software that is now to be found in the **ZX Interface 1**.

Many people have been involved in the **Microdrive** project, but the 'lion's share' of the work has been done by Martin Brennan and Ben Cheese of Sinclair Research Ltd.; and it is to them that the praise should be given.

I would like to record my thanks to Martin, Ben and the other members of the development team for the way they all made me so welcome; and answered so very many questions.

There is no doubt that with the introduction of the **Microdrive** and the **Local Area Network** that personal computing has taken a further leap forward — bringing previously very expensive features to the 'average' person.

It will take some time to develop programs that use the new equipment to its greatest advantage, but Sir Clive Sinclair can be justly proud of the success of his ZX computers.

I would also like to thank
— Alfred Milgrom of Melbourne House (Publishers) for his continuing assistance and advice.
— 'George Tokarski (photographers)' for the photographs.
— Sinclair Research Ltd. for making available early models of the ZX Interface 1 and Microdrives.
— St. Lawrences School, Skellingthorpe, Lincoln, for making available a BBC microcomputer.
and, my wife Liz and daughters — Jackie and Carolyn.

Ian Logan   Lincoln, 1983

Contents

Introduction 1

Chapter 1
The Extended **Spectrum** System 3

Chapter 2
The Extended BASIC 9

Chapter 3
The **Microdrive** 21

Chapter 4
The Local Area Network 43

Chapter 5
The RS232 Link 63

Chapter 6
Using Machine Code
    a. Using the 'Hook Codes' 77
    b. Adding New Statements 91

Index 105

Introduction

The purchase of a **ZX Interface 1** and a **Microdrive** has probably given the average **Spectrum** owner a first introduction to the 'mass storage of data' and 'computer-to-computer linking'. Both these subjects are initially difficult to understand but as with many fields of 'science' the underlying principles are fairly simple.

In this book each facility offered by the **ZX Interface 1** and **Microdrive** will be discussed in turn. Finally the reader is invited to try writing his/her own machine code programs; as it is only with machine code that the system can be made to function to its maximum potential.

Chapter 1

The Extended Spectrum System

The **ZX Interface 1** is a 'communications' board. It allows the **Spectrum** to be linked to **Microdrives**, other **Spectrums** via the **local area network** and **RS232** devices.

A **Spectrum** fitted with a **ZX Interface 1** therefore has the facility to handle:

data coming from: the keyboard
a cassette player
a **Microdrive**
another **Spectrum** (via the network)
an RS232 device

and data going to: a TV
a cassette player
a **Microdrive**
another **Spectrum** (via the network)
an RS232 device
a ZX printer
the on-board loudspeaker

The **Spectrum** system is a single microprocessor system and this has the result of making the 'servicing' of an input or output device a 'dedicated' action. That is to say the **Spectrum** cannot do any other work at the same time as serving an input or output device. The only exception being that the TV signal is produced directly by the Uncommitted Logic Array (U.L.A.) of the **Spectrum**.

Diagram 1 shows the extended **Spectrum** system.

The **ZX Interface 1** can be discussed under three headings:
i   The connectors
ii The 'paging' operation
iii The electronics

Each of these will now be discussed in some detail.

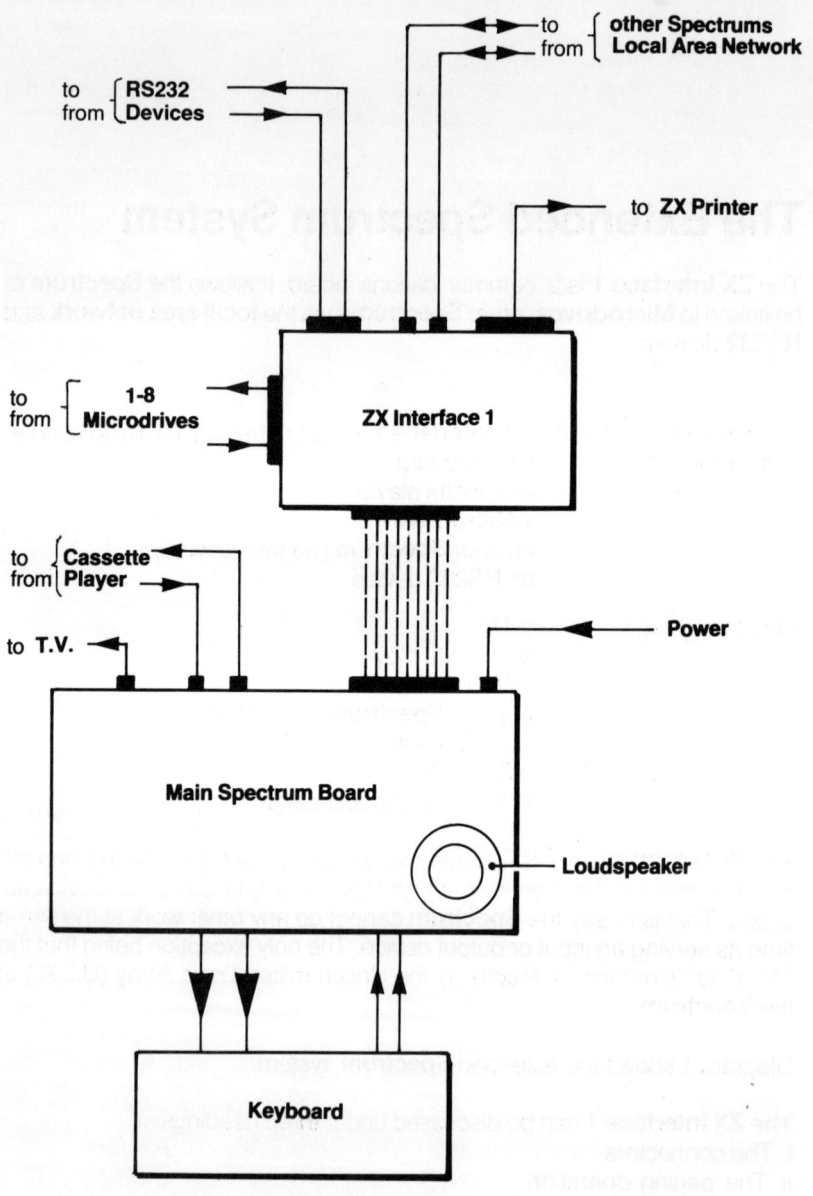

Diagram 1. The extended **Spectrum** system (not to scale).

i. The connectors:
There are five connectors to the printed circuit board of the **ZX Interface 1**.

a. The main edge connector.
This is a 54 track edge connector that joins the **ZX Interface 1** to the **Spectrum** itself. The main 'lines' carried across this connector are the:
- 16 address lines
- 8 data lines
- the ROM chip select line
- +9v., +5v. & 0v.
- M1 (instruction fetch)

but the other control lines are no less important to the operation of the **ZX Interface 1**.

b. The extension connector
The 54 tracks are to the extension connector for using the ZX Printer etc.

c. The Microdrive connector
This is a 14 track connector. The lines are:
- 0v
- +9v.
- Two bidirectional data lines
- R/W (read/write)
- Erase
- Two control lines
- Write protect
- Five unused lines — all grounded.

Data passes between the **ZX Interface 1** and a **Microdrive** in a serial manner — sequential bits being carried on each data line in turn. Port E7h is the input/output port for handling data.

The two control lines are used to select the required **Microdrive** and start/stop its motor. Port EFh is used when handling these lines; as well as the Erase and Write protect lines.

d. The RS232 connector
This is a 9 pin D-socket.
The lines are:

When sending data	— Pin 3 Data out (RXdata)
	— Pin 4 Data terminal ready (DTR)
When receiving data	— Pin 2 Data in (TXdata)
	— Pin 5 Clear to send (CTS)
And, always	— Pin 7 0v.

The **Spectrum** is viewed as a DCE (= data communication equipment) when sending data — a byte of data is sent on RXdata when DTR is found to be high; and vice versa, the **Spectrum** is viewed as a DTE (= data terminal equipment) when receiving data — a byte of data is received on TXdata only when the **Spectrum** has raised CTS to show it is ready.

The port F7h is used by the RS232 link with the data bits being passed serially on data line '0'. The state of the DTR line is found by reading bit 3 of port EFh and the CTS line is raised by setting bit 4 of the same port.

e. The Local Area Network connector

There are a pair of sockets for connecting the user's **Spectrum** to other **Spectrums**. The sockets are identical and there is a pair as this allows a series of **Spectrums** to be chained together without significantly altering the impedance of the network.

The network uses only two lines:
- signal line
- nominal ground

The signal line is set by using data line '0' of port F7h.

Note: The network is dominant to the RS232 link; and the RS232 is selected over the network by having CTS raised (bit 4 of port EFh) during both 'sending' and 'receiving'.

ii. The 'Paging' operation:

The standard **Spectrum** has a 16K ROM (read only memory) that occupies the memory area from address '0' (0000h) to address 16383 (3FFFh). In this ROM are to be found the operating system of the **Spectrum**, the BASIC interpreter, the floating-point calculator and the character set. There is very little in this ROM that applies to the **Microdrive**, Local Area Network or RS232 link.

The ROM program of the standard **Spectrum** has therefore had to be extended to cater for the new devices and this is managed by having a 'shadow' ROM (8K in size) in the **ZX Interface 1**. This second ROM is 'paged' with the original ROM so that at any given moment the **Spectrum** is using one ROM or the other; but never both together.

In the 'shadow' ROM of the **ZX Interface 1** are:
- An extension to the syntax checker to allow for 'new' statements.
- Command routines for the 'new' commands
- Input and output routines for the **Microdrive**, Local Area Network and RS232 link.

The key to understanding how the 'shadow' system actually works, is to appreciate there are operations, which previously led to 'error reports', that are now treated as correct; and the appropriate actions taken.

E.g. The statement — **CAT** 1 — previously gave an error report; but with a **ZX Interface 1** and a **Microdrive** holding a cartridge joined to the **Spectrum** the statement is executed appropriately.

The 'shadow' ROM of the **ZX Interface 1** is selected by performing an instruction-fetch on either location 0008h or location 1708h; and the main ROM is re-selected by an instruction fetch on location 0700h.

There are two routines in the 'shadow' ROM that are worth considering in further detail at this stage.

a. The INSER_ routine

There are '58' extra system variables created when the 'shadow' ROM is paged for the first time after power is connected to the **Spectrum** or a **NEW** command is executed.

This insertion of 'shadow' system variables is handled by the INSER_ routine; as is the initialisation of many of them.

E.g. NTSTAT to '1' — default station '1'

IOBORD to '0' — default I/O colour 'black'

BAUD to '12' — default baud rate = '9600'

b. The CALBAS routine

The CALBAS — call base — routine allows for subroutines in the 'base' (main) ROM of the Spectrum to be called from the 'shadow' ROM. This routine is especially useful as all registers are preserved whilst the 'shadow' ROM is unpaged and paged once again.

The CALBAS routine itself calls the 'ROM paging subroutine' (locations 23737-23746) in the 'shadow' system variables to actually effect the call to the subroutine in the 'base' ROM.

The 'ROM paging subroutine' is:

```
            Org 23737
            H_L Equ 23738
SBRT        LD HL,......     ;the correct value for HL.
            CALL .....       ;the actual subroutine
            LD (H_L),HL      ;save new value of HL.
            RET              ;ready to 'page' again.
```

The locations of H_L are used to 'bring-in' and 'take-out' the value of the HL register pair that would otherwise be corrupted when 'unpaging' and 'paging'.

Hook codes:
The routines of the 'shadow' ROM can be used by the machine code programmer through a series of 'hook codes'. These codes are used after a RST 0008H instruction and will be discussed more fully in the machine code chapter of this book.

iii. The electronics:

The following discussion is not intended to describe the electronic circuitry of the **ZX Interface 1**; but more to describe the functions involved. There are five main functions:

a. The 'paging' mechanism

The 'shadow' ROM has to be selected and de-selected as required. This entails the decoding of the appropriate addresses and the M1 signal. The result is that the signal on the ROM select line ($\overline{\text{ROMCS}}$) is brought high on 'paging' and low on 'unpaging'.

b. Handling the port addresses

The devices attached to the **ZX Interface 1** are selected by using address lines A3 & A4 during input/output instructions. The necessary electronics are therefore required to interpret the signals involved.

c. Handle the data to/from the Microdrive

The bytes of data that are being passed from the **Spectrum** to a **Microdrive** have to pass through a 'parallel-to-serial convertor'. Indeed the bits of a byte also have to be split between the two data lines. The opposite actions are required when receiving data from a **Microdrive**.

d. Handle the data to/from the Local Area Network

The sending of the data over the network is very straightforward but the receiving of data requires that 'hardware' be used to identify the 'falling signal' on the serial data line. This is discussed in further detail in the chapter dealing with the network.

e. Handle the data to/from the RS232 link.

Here it is only necessary to ensure that the correct voltages can be handled.

Most of the electronic circuitry that performs the above operations are contained in a single Uncommitted Logic Array (ULA).

Chapter 2

The Extended BASIC

The fitting of the **ZX Interface 1** to the **Spectrum** has the effect of extending the BASIC syntax checker and interpreter. To the user it therefore appears that the **ZX Interface 1** offers a means by which BASIC statements that were previously not allowed, can now be used.

The extension of the BASIC only applies to statements with the following commands:

> FORMAT
> OPEN #
> CAT
> ERASE
> MOVE
> SAVE, LOAD, VERIFY & MERGE
> CLS & CLEAR

The syntax of the BASIC statements with these commands, together with their actions, will now be described in some detail.

FORMAT:
The syntax for a **FORMAT** statement is:

> FORMAT
> a device expression (M,m,N,n,T,t,B or b)
> a separator (, or ;)
> a numeric expression

and if required

> a separator (, or ;)
> & a naming expression

There are three devices handled by the **ZX Interface 1** — the **Microdrive**, the network & the RS232 link — and for each device a **FORMAT** statement has a specific function.

FORMAT & the Microdrive:
A **FORMAT** statement containing a 'device expression' that is a "M" or a "m" allows the user to **FORMAT** a **Microdrive** cartridge. This formatting action has the effect of giving the user a totally clean cartridge (i.e. all previous information in the cartridge is lost) that is **known** by the 'naming expression'.

Examples of sensible **FORMAT** statements are:

> **FORMAT** "M";1;"First"
> — the cartridge in **Microdrive** '1' will be cleaned and given the name "First".
> **FORMAT** A$;B,C$
> — where A$ is currently "M" or "m"; B is a number in the range 1-8; and C$ is a string with currently 1-10 characters.

The appropriate error message is given if an expression is 'out of range', or there is no 'unprotected' cartridge in the specified **Microdrive** when the statement is executed.

FORMAT & the network:
A **FORMAT** statement containing a 'device expression' that is a "N" or a "n" allows the user to give the **Spectrum** a 'Station number'. When the power is first connected to a **Spectrum** the 'Station number' will always be '1', and the **FORMAT** statement allows the user to change this number as required.

Examples of sensible **FORMAT** statements are:

> **FORMAT** "N";2
> — the 'Station number' is to be '2'.
> **FORMAT** A$;B
> — where A$ is currently "N" or "n"; and B is a number in the range 1-64.

The appropriate error message is given if an expression is 'out of range'; but no error is reported if the user includes in the statement an extra separator and a naming expression — these are simply ignored.

FORMAT & the RS232 link
A **FORMAT** statement containing a 'device expression' that is a "T", "t", "B" or "b" allows the user to specify the baud rate for both input and output operations. By default the baud rate will be '9600' and the **FORMAT** statement allows the user to change the rate between '50' and '19200'. The values allowed are:

50, 110, 300, 600, 1200, 2400, 4800, 9600 & 19200.

Examples of sensible **FORMAT** statements are:
> **FORMAT** "T";1200
> — the baud rate will become '1200'.
> **FORMAT** A$,B
> — where A$ is currently "T", "t", "B" or "b"; and B has a current value.

The appropriate error message will be given if there is an invalid 'device expression' or the baud rate is set to greater than '65535'.

Although the actual settings of the **Spectrum's** baud rate are 'discrete' (9 settings only) no error message is given if 'other' values are used; instead the baud rate 'below' the value is used (with a lower limit of '50').
> e.g. **FORMAT** "t",25000 sets the baud rate to '19200',
> & **FORMAT** "t",.5 sets the baud rate to '50'.

Note that there is no distinction between the actions performed with a statement containing the 'device expression' "B" or one containing "T".

OPEN #:
The syntax for a **OPEN #** statement is:
> **OPEN #**
> a stream number (normally 4-15)
> a separator (, or ;)
> a device expression (M,m,N,n,T,t,B,b)

and if required
> a separator (, or ;)
> a numeric expression

and if required
> a separator (, or ;)
> a naming expression

In the **Spectrum** an **OPEN #** statement has the function of **associating** a specified device with a specified stream; and allows the user to handle the specified device with statements containing the commands:
> **PRINT** #n, **INPUT** #n, & **INKEY$**#n
> where n is the number of the stream associated with the device.

In its default state the **Spectrum** associates the 'keyboard' with streams '0' and '1', the TV screen with stream '2' and the ZX printer with stream '3'. Although it is indeed possible to change the 'associations' of these streams there would appear to be little purpose in so doing.

The actual operation of **OPEN**ing a stream involves two independent steps. First the necessary 'channel data' for the appropriate device is placed in the 'channel information area'. Secondly, the 'offset address' — difference between the base address of the channel data and the system variable CHANS — is placed in the 'streams data area'.

The **OPEN**ing of streams associated with the **Microdrive**, network and RS232 link will now be discussed in turn.

OPEN # & the Microdrive:
An **OPEN #** statement containing a 'device expression' that is a "M" or a "m" allows the user to **associate** a specific stream with a specific named file on a specific **Microdrive**.

Examples of sensible **OPEN #** statements are:

    OPEN #4;"M",1;"FIRST FILE"
    — the file named FIRST FILE on **Microdrive** '1' is to be associated with stream '4'.
    OPEN #A;B$,C,D$(2)
    — where A has a value in the range 0-15; B$ is the expression "M", or "m"; C has a value in the range 1-8; and D$(2) is a string expression with 1-10 characters.

Upon execution of an **OPEN #** statement of this type the file specified will be available for 'writing to' if it is a 'new' file and for 'reading from' if the file already exists. Hence it is not possible in the **Spectrum's Microdrive** system to **add** to an existing file from BASIC.

An error message will be given if the stream is already open (does not apply to streams 0-3), an expression is 'out of range' or there is insufficient memory to allow for the channel information area to be enlarged by 595 bytes.

Note that the use of an **OPEN #** statement to associate a stream with a particular file does not in itself create that file. It is only by writing more than 512 characters to the file, or **CLOSE**ing a stream that has been used, that creates a file.

OPEN # & the network:

An **OPEN** # statement containing a 'device expression' that is a "N" or a "n" allows the user to **associate** a specific stream with the 'sending' or 'receiving' of data over the network to/from a **Spectrum** with a specific station number.

Examples of sensible **OPEN** statements are:

    OPEN #4; "N",44
    — associate stream '4' with a **Spectrum** using the station number '44'.
    OPEN #A,B$,C
    — where A has a value in the range 0-15; B$ is the string expression "N" or "n"; and C has a value in the range 0-64.

Once again error messages will be given upon execution of an **OPEN** # statement of this type if the stream is already open (does not apply to streams 0-3), an expression is 'out of range' or there is insufficient memory to allow for the channel information area to be enlarged by 276 bytes. The association of a given stream with the network does not in itself determine whether the stream is to be used for the sending or the receiving of data; but once a 'network buffer' contains data the **opposite** action is not permissible. I.e. 'received' data can only be 'read' & 'data for sending' can only be 'sent'.

OPEN # & the RS232 link:

An **OPEN** # statement containing a 'device expression' that is a "T", "t", "B" or "b" allows the user to **associate** a specific stream with the RS232 link for either input or output. The baud rate is unaffected by an **OPEN** # statement of this type. Examples of sensible **OPEN** # statements are:

    OPEN #4; "T"
    — stream '4' is associated with RS232 channel data; input & output will be handled as 'text'.
    OPEN #A,B$
    — where A has a value 0-15 and B$ is the expression "B" or "b". Data will be handled in 'binary' mode.

An error message will be given if an expression is 'out of range'. It is unlikely that the report 'Out of memory' will ever be given by using an **OPEN** # statement of this type as the RS232 channel data only uses 11 bytes.

CAT:
The syntax for a **CAT** statement is:
>**CAT**

optionally required
>>a hash sign
>>a stream number
>>a separator (, or ;)

but always
>>a **Microdrive** number

A **CAT** statement simply lists the names of the first 50 unprotected files found in the cartridge in the specified **Microdrive**. The amount of 'free' room in the cartridge is also given. (Names that start with **CHR$** 0 are 'protected' and ignored by a **CAT** statement.)

If no stream number is given in the **CAT** statement then the list will by default be printed to stream '2'; normally the TV screen.

Examples of sensible **CAT** statements are:
>**CAT** 1
>— the list of unprotected files from the cartridge in **Microdrive** '1' is printed to the device associated with stream '2'.
>— **CAT** #A;B
>— where A has a value in the range 0-15 and B a value in the range 1-8.

An error message will be given if an expression is 'out of range', the stream to be used is closed or there is no cartridge in the specified **Microdrive**.

Note that a statement containing only the word **CAT** does pass syntax but will give a run-time error. This occurs as the statement is accepted as correct syntax by the 'original' **Spectrum** ROM program and thereby cannot be 'trapped' by the **ZX Interface 1** until run-time. The use of **CAT** and **ENTER** is therefore an easy way to ensure that 'insertion' of the 'shadow' system variables has been effected.

ERASE:
The syntax for an **ERASE** statement is:
>**ERASE**
>>a device expression (M or m)
>>a **Microdrive** number
>>a naming expression

An **ERASE** statement 'erases' the data blocks in a specified **Microdrive** that currently hold the data belonging to a named file. The data blocks are then 'free' and are ready for further use by another file.

Examples of sensible **ERASE** statements are:
> **ERASE** "M";1;"FIRST_FILE"
> — the file called FIRST_FILE will be erased from the cartridge in **Microdrive**'1'.
> **ERASE** A$;B,C$
> — where A$ is the string expression "M" or "m"; B has a value in the range 1-8; and C$ currently holds the name of a file.

An error report will be given if an expression is 'out of range', or there is no cartridge in the specified **Microdrive**. There is no error if no data blocks for the specified file are to be found.

MOVE:
The syntax for a **MOVE** statement is:
> **MOVE**
> a hash sign
> a stream number
> the keyword **TO**
> a hash sign
> a stream number

As an alternative to a **source** or **destination** being described using a stream it is possible to use a set of channel specifiers, viz.

> a device expression

and if required

> a separator
> a numeric expression

and if required

> a separator
> a naming expression

A **MOVE** statement allows the user to **receive** data from the 'source' stream/channel and **send** the data to a 'destination' stream/channel.

The time taken by a **MOVE** statement has had a 'stream' as a source or a destination, or both, will be no longer than a statement using two sets of channel specifiers.

Examples of sensible **MOVE** statements are:
> **MOVE** #4 **TO** #5
> — where bytes of data 'received' by stream '4' are 'sent' to stream '5'.
> **MOVE** "N";20 **TO** "M";1;"NET_DATA"
> — where bytes of data 'received' over the network from Station 20 are 'sent' to the file NET_DATA.

An error message will be given if an expression is 'out of range'; a stream is closed; there is no cartridge in the specified **Microdrive**; the 'source' file cannot be found; or the 'destination' file already exists.

The **MOVE** command is intended to be used to handle data files that have a **finite** size, i.e. finishing with an 'end of file' declaration. The handling of **infinite** files can lead to problems; as can the handling of BASIC programs or arrays.

SAVE, LOAD, VERIFY & MERGE:

These four commands are used to handle BASIC programs or arrays.

The syntax for a **SAVE, LOAD, VERIFY** or **MERGE** statement is:
> **SAVE/LOAD/VERIFY/MERGE**
> a star
> a device expression (M, m, N, n, T, t, B, b)

and if required
> a separator
> a numeric expression

and if required
> a separator
> a naming expression

and if required one of the following extensions
> ..... (by default a BASIC program)

or
> **LINE**
> a numeric expression (**SAVE**ing an 'auto-run' program)

or
> **DATA**
> an array variable (handling BASIC arrays)

or
> **CODE** (handling a block of data)

and if required
> a numeric expression (the start address)

and if required
> a separator (,)
> a numeric expression (the length of the block)

or
> **SCREEN$** (handling the display file)
> (and attributes file)

The 'star' after the keyword acts as a 'breaker' for the syntax checker of the 'main' ROM and prevents the cassette handling routine being entered in error.

SAVE, LOAD, VERIFY & MERGE statements are used in the same manner in an extended **Spectrum** as in an unexpanded **Spectrum**, with the exception that programs and arrays passed by **Microdrive**, network and RS232 channels do not have names.

Examples of sensible **SAVE** statements are:
> **SAVE** *"m",1,"FIRST_PROG"
> — the current BASIC program in the **Spectrum** is **SAVE**d as file FIRST_PROG on the cartridge in **Microdrive** '1'.
> **SAVE** *"n";2
> — the current BASIC program is passed over the network to be received by Station '2'.
> **SAVE** *"b" **SCREEN$**
> — the current display file (& attributes file) is sent out on the RS232 link. (**SAVE**ing with the device expression "t" is illogical and leads to a run-time error.)

Examples of sensible **LOAD** statements are:
> **LOAD** *"m";4,"FOUR_PROG"
> — the file FOUR_PROG will be **LOAD**ed — as long as it exists and is indeed a BASIC program.
> **LOAD** *"n";33
> — a program from Station '33' is **LOAD**ed.
> **LOAD** *"b"
> — a BASIC program is **LOAD**ed from the RS232 link.

Note that it is just possible for 'data', being received via the network or RS232 link to be 'recognised' initially as a BASIC program. In such a case the **Spectrum** is liable to 'crash'; rather than give the report 'Wrong file type'.

Examples of sensible **VERIFY** statements are:

VERIFY *"M",4;"FOUR_PROG"
— compare the file FOUR_PROG against the current program in the **Spectrum**
VERIFY *"N";33
— compare the 'second' copy of a BASIC program against the 'first'; allows nicely for 'echoing' over the network.
VERIFY *"B" **CODE** 32000,256
— check the bytes presently in the memory against the data being received via the RS232 link.

Examples of sensible **MERGE** statements are:

MERGE *"m";1;"PART_TWO"
— the BASIC program PART_TWO is **MERGE**d with the current program.
MERGE *"n";33
— the program being received from Station '33' is **MERGE**d with the current program.
MERGE *"b"
— the program being received via the RS232 link is **MERGE**d with the current program.

Remember that only BASIC programs and their variables can be **MERGE**d; otherwise the report — '**MERGE** error' — will be given. Also note that 'auto-run' BASIC programs will not **MERGE** unless being loaded from a cassette.

CLS & CLEAR:

As a 'bonus' to the user of the **ZX Interface 1** the BASIC has been extended to include the two statements:

CLS #
CLEAR #

CLS #:

The statement **CLS #** performs the actions associated with the 'original' **CLS** — in that the display file and the attributes area are 'cleared' — but in addition 'resets':

INK to BLACK
PAPER to WHITE
BORDER to WHITE
INVERSE to 'no'
BRIGHT to 'no'
OVER to 'no'
FLASH to 'no'

The statement **CLS #** thereby 'clears the screen fully'.

CLEAR #:

The statement **CLEAR #** 'clears the stream data area'. All streams are **CLOSE**d — streams '0'-'3' are given their 'normal' values and streams '4'-'15' have their stream data bytes made zero. If there is any 'unsent' data found in a channel area buffer then it is discarded (in contrast to **CLOSE #**) as the channel area is reduced to its minimum configuration.

The user may also define new BASIC statements — along the lines of **CLS #** & **CLEAR #** — in an extended **Spectrum**. Details of how this can be done will be found in the machine code part of this book.

A note on stream selection:
In the **Spectrum** an output stream will stay 'selected' from one BASIC statement to another. This action is of no detriment in the standard **Spectrum** but in the extended **Spectrum** it can account for the non-execution of certain statements.

E.g. Try: **CLS #: PAPER** 2: **CLS**
— and the main screen does go red.
but: **CLS #: SAVE** *"n";0: **PAPER** 2: **CLS**
— and it does **not**.

The remedy is to select the main screen before using **PAPER, CLS, INK** etc.

E.g. **CLS #: SAVE** *"n";0: **PRINT** ;: **PAPER** 2: **CLS**
— and this re-selects the main screen. The statement **PRINT** ; is a 'dummy' statement.

Chapter 3

The Microdrive

AUTHOR'S NOTE:
Sinclair Research Ltd. has requested that details that might compromise the 'security' of the **Microdrive** are not to be published; hence in this chapter there are certain points which are not discussed as fully as they might have been. There remains, however, much that the reader should find of great interest.

Introduction:
The **Microdrive** system is essentially a mini-cassette system; and can be considered in four separate parts.

The Microdrive Units
The actual **Microdrives** are best described as specially manufactured mini-cassette players. Up to eight such units can be linked together at any one time and controlled from a **Spectrum** fitted with a **ZX Interface 1**. Each **Microdrive** unit has a slot to receive a cartridge, a drive motor, two sets of REAQD/WRITE/ERASE heads and the necessary electronics to allow the unit to function.

The Microdrive Cartridges
A cartridge contains a single piece of recording tape of length 200 inches (= 5m.) and width 1/16th. of an inch (= 1.5mm.). There is a single 'splice' and the tape thereby appears continuous. The tape is driven by a 'pinch wheel' mechanism and feeds from the 'centre', goes past the recording heads before being taken up on the 'outside' of its single spool.

The Microdrive connectors
The first drive unit is connected to the **ZX Interface 1** by a 16 track ribbon cable. Two or more drive units are joined to each other by 16 track connectors.

The ZX Interface 1
This unit contains:

a. The software necessary to extend the BASIC so as to allow the **Microdrive** system to be controlled.

b. The hardware necessary to handle the control signals and to serialize/deserialize the data that passes between a **Spectrum** and a **Microdrive** unit.

Using the Microdrive system:

A **Microdrive** cartridge is capable of holding, on average, 90K of data. This data can be made up of 'program files' or 'data files'. A single cartridge may hold from one to about one hundred and eighty files at any one time and it is perfectly permissible to have both program and data files on a tape at the same time. Each file must have a unique name of between one and ten characters. All characes are allowed including tokens. To the user it appears that a cartridge holds 'named files' of varying sizes, but in reality a tape is 'sectored' with each sector holding a block of data of up to 512 bytes.

Note: A cartridge holds a tape of length 200 inches. There are almost 200 sectors on each tape. Therefore a sector is about 1 inch of tape, i.e. there is a data-density of about 500 bytes/inch. (See later in the chapter for more details.).

A 'named file' will use just a single sector if the length of the file is less than 512 bytes; and more than one sector if longer. Note that a sector can only be associated with one 'named file' at a time whether the sector is fully used or not. The sectors that hold parts of a 'named file' form the 'records' for that file. These records are numbered 0,1,...,n.

The facilities offered to the user by the **Microdrive** system will now be discussed in turn.

FORMATting a cartridge:

A new cartridge must be prepared for use by executing the statement:

      FORMAT "m";1;"...name..."
      — with the cartridge in drive '1'.

This statement has three effects:
    1. The tape is fully erased.
    2. The tape is 'sectored' (and verified).
    3. The cartridge's name is written to each sector that is created.

CATaloguing a cartridge:
At any time the user may ask for a catalogue of the files in a particular cartridge by using the statement:

> **CAT** 1
> — with the cartridge in drive '1'. The catalogue appears on the TV screen

Also:

> **CAT #4**;1
> — catalogue to be **PRINT**ed to stream '4'.

The catalogue is given as:
> The cartridge's name.
> A list of the first fifty names of the files found on the cartridge. (Arranged in character-code order.)
> The remaining free space on the cartridge — given in K.

Note that filenames are given without any indication as to the nature of the file. Also, filenames which begin with '**CHR$** 0' are not displayed.

ERASEing a file:
Any file may be erased by using the statement:

> **ERASE** "m";1;"...name..."
> — with the cartridge in drive '1'.

This operation will be very slow (about 40 seconds) if there is no 'end of file' record to be found.

Handling BASIC programs, named arrays or blocks of data:

SAVEing 'program files':
'Program files' are created by the use of the **SAVE** command.

E.g.

> **SAVE** *"m";1;"PROG_ONE"
> — A 'program file' named 'PROG_ONE' is created on the cartridge in drive '1'.
> **SAVE** *"m";2;"SC_ONE" **SCREEN$**
> — A 'program file' named 'SC_ONE' is created on the cartridge in drive '2'.

> **SAVE** *"m";3;"ARRAY_1" **DATA** A()
> — A 'program file' named 'ARRAY_1' is created on the cartridge in drive '3'.

From these examples it can be seen that 'program files' do not necessarily only hold BASIC programs and their variables; but may hold named arrays or blocks of code (viz. the cassette system of the **Spectrum**).

If a BASIC program is to be executed directly on **LOAD**ing then it has to be **SAVE**d with a line number.

E.g.

> **SAVE** *"m";1;"PROG_TWO" **LINE** 10
> — When subsequently **LOAD**ed the program will be executed directly from line 10.

Note that in all cases when **SAVE** is used the 'new' file must be given a name that does not already exist on the cartridge.

VERIFYing 'program files':
As with the cassette system of the **Spectrum** the user may **VERIFY** a program once it has been **SAVE**d.
E.g.

> **VERIFY** *"m";1;"PROG_ONE"
> — the present program and its variables are compared to the contents of the file 'PROG_ONE'.

LOADing and MERGEing 'program files':
'Program files' can be fetched by using the **LOAD** and **MERGE** commands. E.g.

> **LOAD** *"m";1;"PROG_ONE"
> — The file 'PROG_ONE' is taken from the cartridge in drive '1' and becomes the current program.
> **LOAD** *"m";2;"SC_ONE" **SCREEN$**
> — The file 'SC_ONE', which must be a 'block of code' is **LOAD**ed into the appropriate memory locations.
> **MERGE** *"m";3;"PROG_THREE"
> — The file 'PROG_THREE' is **MERGE**d with the current program.

Note that a BASIC program **SAVE**d with a **LINE** number will be executed directly after **LOAD**ing; and such a program cannot be **MERGE**d. Also note that pressing the **BREAK** key whilst **LOAD**ing causes a total system restart.

Handling 'data files':

In contrast to the cassette system of the **Spectrum** which only allows for the use of 'program files', the **Microdrive** system can handle 'data files'.

'Data files' are always serial access files; although the user can produce the illusion of random access filing, if wished, by reading a file completely, amending it as required and storing the file again.

Producing a 'data file':

The production of a 'data file' involves the use of **OPEN, PRINT** and **CLOSE** statements.

The **OPEN** statement has to be used first and has the form:

    10 **OPEN** #4;"m";1;"...name..."
    — the data-items will be 'sent' along stream '4' to the **Microdrive** file.

The actual command routine of the **OPEN** command creates a **Microdrive** channel' in the channel information area. This channel is then associated with stream '4'. The most important part of the channel is the data buffer which occupies 512 locations and can therefore hold 512 bytes of data before becoming full.

The data buffer is filled by using **PRINT** statements. E.g.

    20 **FOR** A=1 TO 300
    30 **PRINT** #4;A
    40 **NEXT** A

Then, once the data-items have been declared the stream should be **CLOSE**d. E.g.

    50 **CLOSE** #4

The actual file on the **Microdrive** cartidge is created when the data buffer in the channel information area is emptied for the first time. This may occur either when the data buffer is filled for the first time or, with a partially filled data buffer; when the **CLOSE** statement is executed. As occurs when using 'program files' a file will only be created if a 'new' filename is being used.

The bytes of data 'sent' from the data buffer to the **Microdrive** file will be placed in a fresh sector of the cartridge, thereby forming a new record for that file. The 'record descriptor', i.e. the header of the record, holds the filename and the 'number of the buffer' being sent. The data 'sent' when the **CLOSE** statement is executed forms the final record of a file and is marked 'end-of-file'. The **CLOSE** statement also leads to the **Microdrive** channel bytes being reclaimed.

Reading a 'data file':
The reading of a 'data file' involves the use of **OPEN, INPUT** and/or **INKEY$**, and **CLOSE** statements.

As with producing a 'data file' the **OPEN** statement has to be used first. E.g.

      10 **OPEN** #4;"m";1;"...name..."

This type of statement once again creates a '**Microdrive** channel' associated with a specified stream.

The subsequent use of an **INPUT** or an **INKEY$** statement for the first time leads to the first record of the named file being copied into the data buffer. Further records are collected as required until the record marked 'end-of-file' is found.

A statement such as:

      20 **INPUT** #4;A

takes bytes in order from the data buffer until a carriage-return character is found. The bytes are then assigned to the variable. Note the similarity to the manner in which the user responds to an ordinary **INPUT** statement by pressing keys on the keyboard, finishing with **ENTER**.

Strings of characters can be assigned to string variables as with:

      30 **INPUT** #4;A$

As with a numeric variable all characters before the carriage-return character are assigned to the variable.

The use of the **INKEY$** function is just a little different in that a single character is returned to the user on every occasion **INKEY$** is used.

      E.g. 40 **PRINT INKEY$**#4;
           – will lead to the printing of a single character read from the file.

The use of a **CLOSE** statement leads to the channel bytes being reclaimed thereby losing any data that might have been 'unread'.

Note that the report 'End of file' will be given if the user should attempt to 'read' non existent bytes from a file.

The following annotated program illustrates the points made above about producing and reading a 'data file'.

Producing a file:
```
10 OPEN #12;"m";1;"Alphabet" – create a Microdrive channel.
20 FOR A=65 TO 90
30 PRINT #12;A – enter 26 numbers into the data buffer.
40 NEXT A
50 CLOSE #12 – 'send' the data-items and reclaim the Microdrive
                channel bytes.
```

Reading a file:
```
60  OPEN #14;"M";1;"Alphabet" – create a Microdrive channel.
70  FOR B=1 TO 1000 — Read the file until its end.
80  INPUT #14;C
90  PRINT CHR$ C; — print each ASCII character.
100 NEXT B
```

And; after the report 'end of file'

CLEAR# or **CLOSE #14**

to close down the open stream.

In the above program the 'data file' — Alphabet — contains a set of printed-numbers;

> i.e. The number 'ten' occupies three bytes, a '1', a '0' and a 'carriage return'.

But, a 'data file' to hold the alphabet might equally well have twenty six single character string items, or a single string of all the characters.

MOVEing 'data files':

In the **Microdrive** system it is not possible to **MOVE** 'program files'; i.e. files created by using **SAVE**.

However, any 'data file' can be **MOVE**d and this can be most useful as it provides a method by which 'data files' can be copied with ease.

E.g. To make a copy of the file — Alphabet, with the new file to be named — Letters:
MOVE "m";1;"Alphabet" **TO** "m";1;"Letters"

Also, the **MOVE** command can be used to pass the bytes of a 'data file' between **Microdrive** and another device. There are many possible examples that can be discussed but perhaps the most useful are the following simple statements:

MOVE "m";1;"Alphabet" **TO** #2
& **MOVE** "m";1;"Alphabet" **TO** #3

which allows the user to obtain a print-out, on the screen or the ZX printer, of the items held in a 'data file'.

The technical details of the Spectrum Microdrive system:

The **Microdrive** system will now be discussed under three headings:

— the tape format
— the **Microdrive** channel
— the BASIC command routines

There will not, however, be any discussion on the electronics of the system; and machine code details will be left until later in the book.

The tape format:

All data is stored on a **Microdrive** tape using two tracks — with data bits being stored alternatively on each track. This 2-track system means that a data bit can 'occupy' a longer length of tape than if a single track were used — for a given speed. Of course a **Microdrive** unit now has to have a double set of recording heads and data has to be handled in two streams; but the gain in operating speed is impressive.

Diagram 1 shows how data bits can be visualised as existing on a **Microdrive** tape.

It will be sensible from now on to ignore the fact that 2 tracks are actually used and consider that bytes of data are stored discretely on a tape in a serial manner. This is shown in diagram 2.

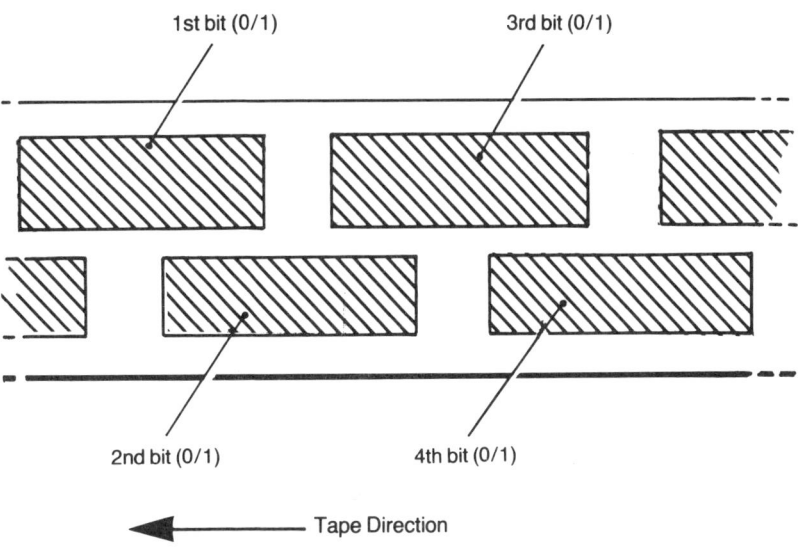

Diagram 1. The storage of data-bits on a **Microdrive** tape.

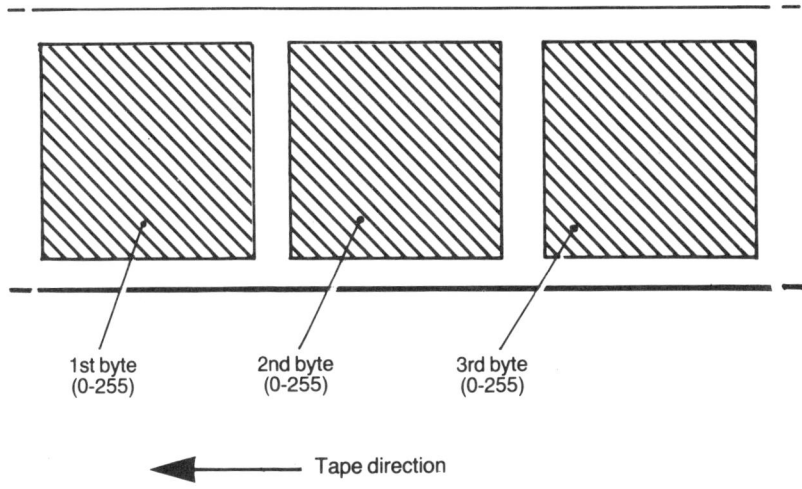

Diagram 2. The storage of data-bytes on a **Microdrive** tape.
(Note: The longitudinal scale has been compressed about 10 fold; as compared to diagram 1.)

A block of data bytes starts with a 'preamble' of twelve bytes. This 'preamble' has ten bytes of '0' and two bytes of '255' and enables the hardware of the system to identify the start of a block of data bytes with great accuracy.

The operation of **FORMAT**ting a cartridge divides the tape into sectors each of which has the following parts:

— **A header block**
   with: a) Twelve bytes of preamble
              b) A sector header — fifteen bytes as follows:
- A flag byte
- A sector number byte
- Two unused bytes
- Ten bytes for the current cartridge name
- A checksum byte

— **A first gap**

— **A data block**
   with: a) Twelve bytes of preamble
              b) A record descriptor — fifteen bytes as follows:
- A flag byte
- A record number byte
- Two bytes for the 'record length'.
- Ten bytes for the current filename
- A checksum byte

              c) A record
- '512' byte data area
- A checksum byte

— **A second gap**

An approximate guide to the relative sizes of the parts is given by the following timings:
— header block — 1.25 ms
— first gap — 3.75 ms
— data block — 25 ms
— second gap — 7 ms

Diagram 3 shows the sectoring of a **Microdrive** tape. The diagram illustrates, also, how roughly two-thirds of the tape can be used to hold data in the normal operating manner.

Diagram 4 shows how the sectors of a **Microdrive** tape might be used by a set of files.

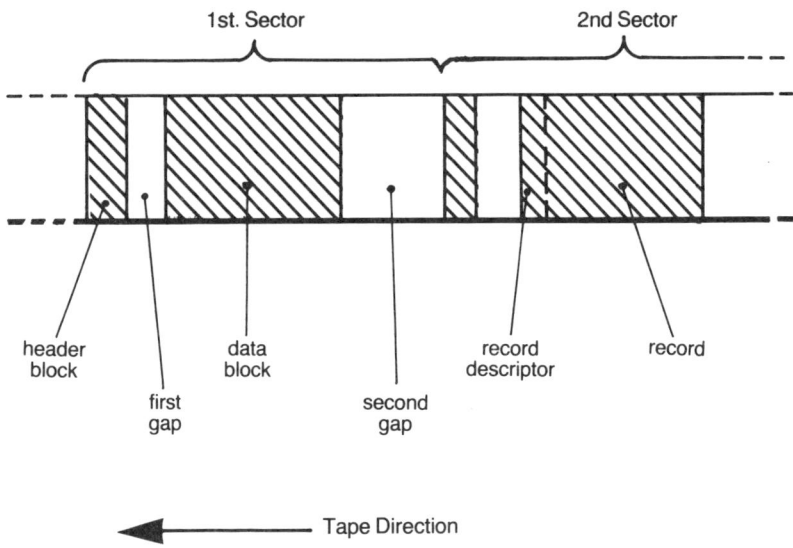

Diagram 3. 'Sectors' on a **Microdrive** tape ('preambles' are not shown).

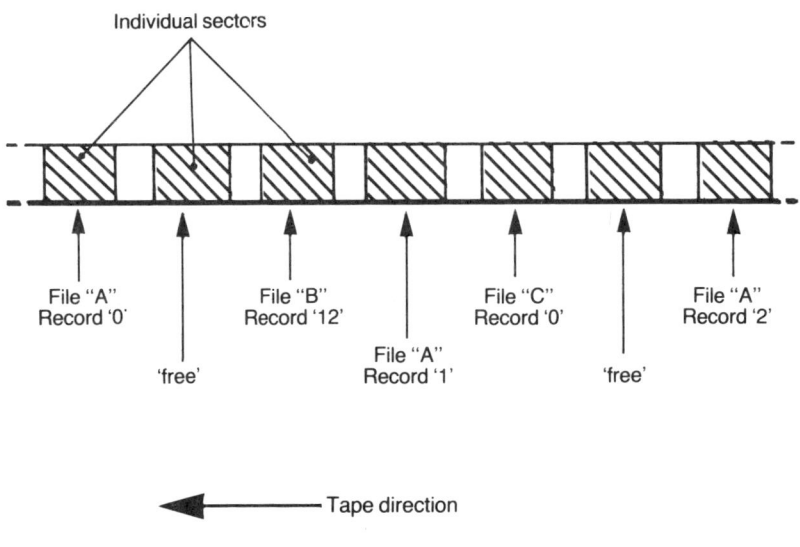

Diagram 4. 'Files' on a **Microdrive** tape.

The Microdrive channel:

All communication of data between a **Spectrum** and a **Microdrive** unit is handled through a **Microdrive** channel. The most important part of the channel being the five hundred and twelve byte data buffer.

The user can request the creation of a channel by using an **OPEN** statement, in which case a specific stream is associated with the channel. However, on many occasions a **Microdrive** channel is created in an 'ad hoc' manner; for example when **SAVE**ing a program a channel is created and used to transfer the necessary bytes of data from the **Spectrum** to the **Microdrive** cartridge.

A **Microdrive** channel has the following format:

bytes	contents	
0-1	Address 0008h.	
2-3	Address 0008h.	
4	"M"	("M" + 80h if 'ad hoc')
5-6	Address MWRCH	(output subroutine address)
7-8	Address MRDCH	(input subroutine address)
9-10	Number '595'	(length of **Microdrive** channel)
11-12	CHBYTE	(counter for data area)
13	CHREC	(buffer number — starts at zero)
14-23	CHNAME	(characters of filename)
24	CHFLAG	(read/write flag)
25	CHDRIV	(number of **Microdrive** unit)
26-27	CHMAP	(address of current map)

;the following '27' locations form the Header block work space

28-39	Header block preamble	
40	HDFLAG	(flag byte)
41	HDNUMB	(sector number)
42-43	Unused	
44-53	HDNAME	(cartridge name)
54	HDCHK	(checksum for previous fourteen bytes)

;the following '540' locations form the Data block work space.

55-66	Data block preamble	
67	RECFLG	(flag byte)
68	RECNUM	(buffer number)
69-70	RECLEN	(current buffer length)
71-80	RECNAM	(characters of filename)
81	DESCHK	(checksum for previous fourteen bytes)
82-593	The data area of 512 locations.	
594	DCHK	(checksum of data area).

The manner in which the above listed locations of the **Microdrive** channel are used will now be discussed by considering the command routines of the various BASIC commands that use the **Microdrive** system. The reader will also find it useful to refer to diagram 5 — the 'writing' and 'reading' of records.

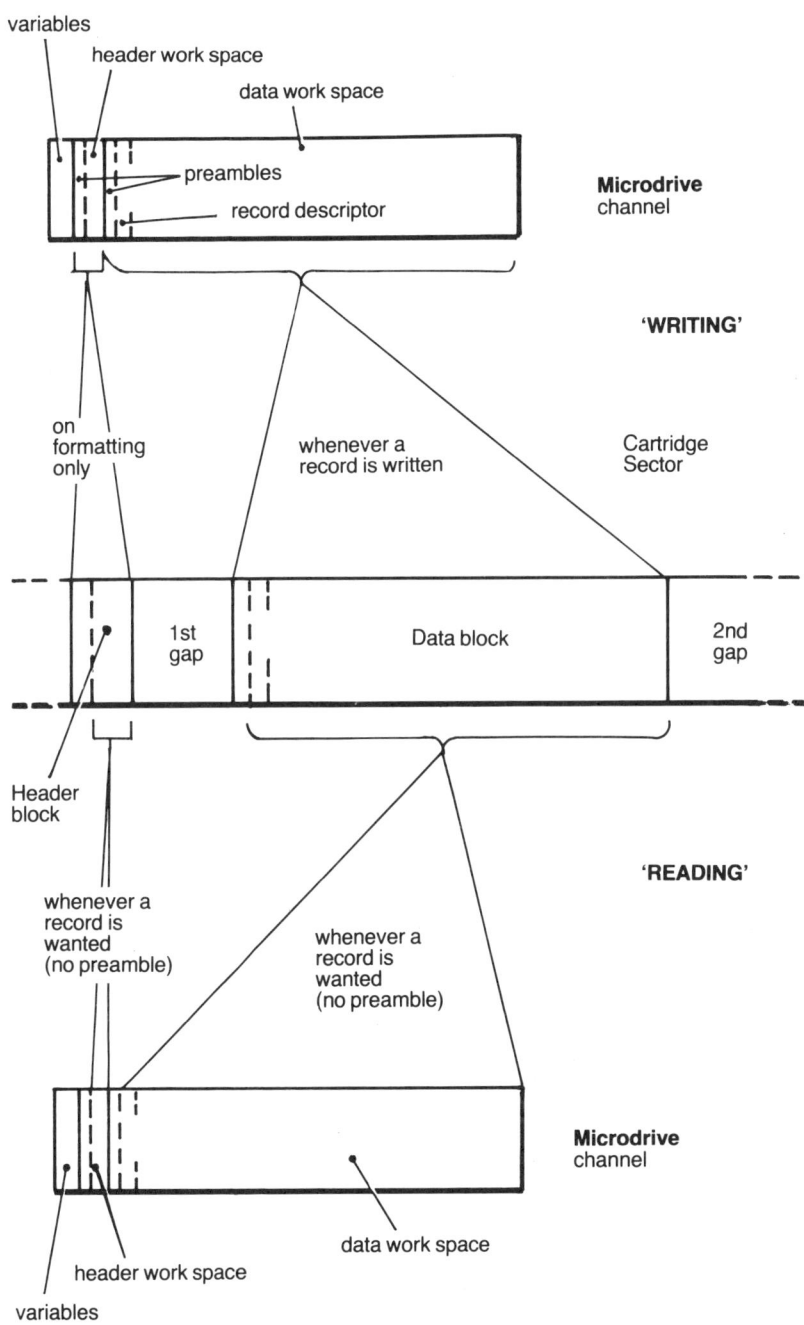

Diagram 5. The 'writing' and 'reading' of records.

The BASIC command routines:
In this section the actual coding is not going to be discussed but only an outline of the actions that are followed by the routines. In this way it is hoped that the user obtains a clear understanding of the functioning of the **Microdrive** system.

— FORMAT
The operation of **FORMAT**ting a cartridge must obviously be the first operation to be discussed, although it is rather complicated.

The steps involved are:

i. An 'ad hoc' channel is created for communication between the **Spectrum** and **Microdrive** unit.
The drive number goes into the location CHDRIV and the cartridge name into the locations of CHNAME.

ii. A '**Microdrive** map' is prepared in the 'map area', i.e. between the system variables area and the channel information area.

> — A **Microdrive** map occupies '32' locations and is used to hold '256' flags that show which sectors of a cartridge are free for use.

All the bits of the map are initialised to '1' — 'in use'.

iii. The motor of the **Microdrive** unit, as indicated by the value in the CHDRIV, is started.

iv. The bytes of the Header work space are initialised.

v. The '540' bytes of the Data block are initialised. (The data area holding test data.)

vi. Now the actual 'sectors' can be created on the tape. The Header block bytes are copied from the Header work space (27 bytes) and the Data block bytes are copied from the Data block work space (540 bytes). In total '255' sectors are created with normally the last '60' or so sectors overwriting the first ones.
The sectors are numbered from '255' downwards.

vii. The 'test data' is now checked by reading back all the records. If the checksum for a record proves correct then the appropriate bit in the **Microdrive** map is reset — free for use.

viii. A second 'writing' operation is now performed with zeroes being held by RECFLAG & RECLEN. The 'writing' is performed to all sectors currently marked 'free for use' and in this manner all sectors that are in working order are made available for files.

ix. The **Microdrive** unit's motor is turned off.

x. The **Microdrive** channel is reclaimed.

— CAT

The steps involved in producing a catalogue of the files on a cartridge area are as follows:

i. The required stream is made the 'current stream'. (By default stream '2' is used.)

ii. An 'ad hoc' **Microdrive** channel is created.

iii. A '**Microdrive** map' is prepared. As with **FORMAT** the '256' bits are all set — in use.

iv. The motor of the **Microdrive** unit, as indicated by the value in CHDRIV, is started.

v. Now all the 'sectors' of the cartridge are examined in turn.

IF the sector is 'free for use' **THEN** the appropriate bit in the **Microdrive** map is reset; **ELSE** the filename of the sector is considered for entry into a list of filenames that is built up in the data area. Only new filenames are entered; and filenames starting with **CHR$** 0 are ignored. All entries are re-ordered as a new name is added. Only 50 filenames are collected.
The cartridge's name will be found every time a sector Header block is identified and loaded into the Header work space of the channel.

vi. The results of making the catalogue are now printed:

— the cartridge name, from HDNAME.
— the various filenames, from the data area.
— the amount of 'free room', found by examining the map, counting the number of reset bits and dividing the answer by two.

viii. The **Microdrive** channel and map are reclaimed.

— ERASE

The steps involved in **ERASE**ing a named file from a **Microdrive** cartridge are as follows:

i. An 'ad hoc' **Microdrive** channel and a map are created.

ii. The motor of the **Microdrive** unit, as indicated by the value in CHDRIV, is started.

iii. The first '32' locations of the data area are set to zero. These bytes will be treated as a map that will 'list' the sectors to be 'reclaimed'.

iv. A counter is initialised to '1280'; this will be used to count the sectors.
— i.e. at least five passes around the tape if necessary.

v. Now the record descriptors from all the sectors of the tape are fetched in turn.

IF a sector holds a record of the file **THEN** the appropriate bit in the 'list' is set.
ELSE the sector is ignored.

If the sector holding the 'end of file' record is found then the record number is copied into the location CHREC.

Sectors will be examined until either the sector-counter reaches zero or the number of records found for the file equals the number in CHREC.

vi. A further pass of the tape now occurs. On this passage 'free for use' record descriptors are written to the sectors that have been marked for erasure in the 'list'.

vii. The **Microdrive** unit's motor is turned off.

viii. The **Microdrive** channel and map are reclaimed.

— SAVE
This command is the first of the set of commands that 'write' data to the **Microdrive** cartridge. In all cases a **Microdrive** map has to be built up for the cartridge being used in order to show which sectors are free for use. Also, the filenames that are already declared have to be compared to the new filename to ensure the new filename is indeed unique.

The actual steps are:

i. An 'ad hoc' **Microdrive** channel and a map are created.

ii. The motor of the **Microdrive** unit, as indicated by the value in CHDRIV, is started.

iii. All the sectors of the cartridge are examined in turn. A **Microdrive** map is built up to show which, if any, sectors are free for use; and the filenames are checked to ensure the new filename can be used.

iv. A 'header' of nine bytes that describe the 'program' are transferred to the data area of the **Microdrive** channel.

These header-bytes describe the 'program' in a similar fashion to that used in the cassette system:

    viz. byte 1 — a code byte
          0 = BASIC program
          1/2 = Named arrays
          3 = Code blocks
    bytes 2&3 — the length of the block.
    bytes 4&5 — the starting address of the block.
    bytes 6&7 — the length of a program alone.
    bytes 8&9 — the line number if **LINE** is used.

v. The bytes that form the 'program' are now transferred to the data area of the **Microdrive** channel. But, whenever the data area is full (actually when trying to transfer a 513th byte) it has to be copied to the **Microdrive** cartridge. This operation involves:

    — Finding the Header block of the next sector on the tape.
    — Examining the **Microdrive** map to see if the sector is 'free for use'. If it is not then the next sector is considered.
    — Copying the '540' bytes from the data block work space on to the tape — forming a new record.
    — Setting the appropriate bit for the sector in the **Microdrive** map to show that the sector is now 'in use'.

The value in RECNUM — the buffer counter — is incremented every time the operation is performed.

vi. An 'end of file' record is now created. This involves setting the 'end of file' flag in RECFLAG and copying, for the final time, the '540' bytes of the data block work space to a new sector on the tape.

vii. The **Microdrive** unit's motor is turned off.

viii. The **Microdrive** channel is reclaimed.

— LOAD, VERIFY & MERGE

The command routines for these three commands are identical in respect to the **Microdrive** software, so they can be considered together.

The steps are:

i. An 'ad hoc' **Microdrive** channel and a map are created.

ii. The motor of the **MIcrodrive** unit, as indicated by the value in CHDRIV, is started.

iii. The data block of the sector that holds the first record of the 'program' is copied into the work space.

iv. The first nine bytes of the 'program' are taken to hold the header information and this is interpreted in the appropriate manner — depends on the command being used and the type of 'program'. The remainder of the first buffer is then **LOAD**ed, **VERIFY**ed or **MERGE**d.

v. The other sectors that hold the various records of the 'program' are fetched in the correct order; until a record marked 'end of file' is found.

vi. The **Microdrive** unit's motor is turned off.

vii. The **Microdrive** channel and map are reclaimed.

— OPEN

Many of the steps performed by the **OPEN** command routine are different depending on whether the user wishes to 'read' an existing file or 'write' a new file. Remember it is not possible to 'write' any additional data to an existing file in the **Spectrum Microdrive** system.

The steps are:

i. A **Microdrive** channel is created. It is associated with the stream specified in S_STR1, the **Microdrive** unit specified in D_STR1 and the filename in N_STR1.

ii. The motor of the **Microdrive** unit, as indicated by the value in CHDRIV, is started.

iii. All the sectors of the tape are now examined in turn. A **Microdrive** map is built up to show which sectors are 'free for use' — will be used later if 'writing' a file. Also, all declared filenames are compared against the present filename.

iv. — for writing a file.

If no sectors are found with the same filename as the new name then it is presumed that the user wishes to 'write' a new file. In this case there is a jump to step v.

— for 'reading' an existing file.

In the case of an existing file being found then the appropriate flags are set to show that the user wishes to 'read'; and the first record of the file is copied into the data work space of the **Microdrive** channel.

v. The **Microdrive** unit's motor is turned off.

— PRINT (to a Microdrive stream)
In the Spectrum system the execution of a **PRINT** statement has the effect of 'sending' a series of character codes to a specified device. The device is identified by its being the object device of the 'current' stream. Therefore when the user enters — **PRINT #5**; . . . (for example), the characters will be sent to the appropriate output routine. In the case of a **Microdrive** stream the routine is named MWRCH (= **Microdrive** write character).

The action of the MWRCH routine is to add a single character code to the buffer of the current **Microdrive** channel; but on every occasion that the buffer is found 'full' then the contents of the buffer are copied to the next 'free' sector on the appropriate **Microdrive** tape, thereby forming a new record for the file. The buffer counter (and therefore the record number) is incremented every time a buffer is copied. Note that an 'end of file' record can never be created by the use of **PRINT** statements.

— INKEY$ (from a Microdrive stream)
The action of the **INKEY$** function complements that of the **PRINT** command.
On every occasion a character code is required, a call is made to the MRDCH routine (= **Microdrive** read character). This routine returns a single character code from the buffer of the appropriate **Microdrive** channel; but whenever the buffer is found to be empty then the next record of the file has to be fetched from the appropriate **Microdrive** tape. The report 'end of file' will be given if the present buffer is both empty and the 'end of file' flag is already set.

— INPUT (from a Microdrive stream)
The execution of an **INPUT** statement is effected by making repeated use of the MRDCH routine. Single characters are fetched and stored in the Editing Area until a 'carriage return' character is found; then the **INPUT** characters are assigned to the specified variable.

— CLOSE
The steps involved in **CLOSE**ing a **Microdrive** stream are:

i. Examine the value held in CHFLAG associated with the stream. **IF** the value is zero **THEN** the channel is being used for 'reading'; and all that is required for the channel to be reclaimed — any unused data in the buffer is lost. **ELSE** the channel is being used for 'writing'; and the following steps are performed.

ii. the appropriate bit of RECFLAG is set to show that an 'end of file' record is to be created.

iii. The motor of the **Microdrive** unit, as indicated by the value in CHDRIV, is started.

iv. Each sector header is examined until a free sector is identified (by reference to the current map from the channel).

v. An 'end of file' record is entered into the sector.

vi. The **Microdrive** unit's motor is turned off.

vii. The **Microdrive** channel and map are reclaimed.

— MOVE

The command routine for this command is rather complicated as there are so many devices that may be specified in the **MOVE** statement. However, the basis of the **MOVE** operation is the use, repeatedly, of first a 'read' routine followed by a 'write' routine.

The following example shows this in a short program.

> The statement **MOVE** "m";1;"a" **TO** "m";1;"b" can be affected by:
> 10 **OPEN** #4;"m";1;"a"
> 20 **OPEN** #5;"m";1;"b"
> 30 **PRINT** #5;**CHR$ INKEY$**#4; **GO TO** 30
> but upon execution it will finish with the 'end of file' report — as the length of the file is not specified.

A note about COPIES:

It is possible by using, for example — **POKE** 23791,20 — before a **SAVE** command to make multiple copies of the records for the program being **SAVE**d. This operation, of course, devotes a lot more of a cartridge to a single program; but when **LOAD**ing the program subsequently there will be an impressive saving in the time taken to locate the first, and other, records of the program.

Looking at records & sectors:

The following pair of BASIC programs show how with a 'data file' it is possible to find the sector-numbers used by the records of the file.

> 10 **OPEN** #4;"m";1;"a"
> 20 **FOR** A=1 **TO** 3000
> 30 **PRINT** #4;**CHR$** 65;
> 40 **NEXT** A
> 50 **CLOSE** #4

The above BASIC lines create a file named "a" that holds '3000' A's.

The file "a" can now be read using:
```
     NEW
  10 OPEN #4;"m";1;"a"
  20 PRINT "Record";PEEK 23912,"Sector";PEEK 23885
  30 POKE 23856,3
  40 LET A$=INKEY$#4
  50 GO TO 20
```
NOTES:
The initial **NEW** ensures the **Microdrive** channel is fixed at location 23844 and onwards.

The record-number is read from the data work space and the sector-number from the header work space.

The **POKE** 23856,3 puts a high value into CHBYTE and in effect empties the data buffer.

On the author's machine the following results were obtained for file "a":

```
          Record 0   Sector 162
          Record 1   Sector 154
          Record 2   Sector 146
          Record 3   Sector 138
          Record 4   Sector 129
          Record 5   Sector 121 (End of file record)
```

Looking at Microdrive maps:

Very little has been said about **Microdrive** maps in the discussion so far because the user never has to manipulate the contents of a map area. However it is interesting to examine a **Microdrive** map; and the following BASIC program shows how this can be done.

— Start by **FORMAT**ting a tape, e.g. **FORMAT** "m",1,"map"
— use **NEW** & **ENTER**, so as to clear any existing maps and channels
— Enter:
```
  10 OPEN #4;"m",1;"any" — a new file
  20 FOR A=23792 TO 23823 — the map for 'any'
  30 LET N=PEEK A — each byte
  40 FOR B=1 TO 8 — 8 bits to a byte
  50 PRINT N/2<> INT(N/2); — each bit a '0' or '1'
  60 LET N=INT (N/2)
  70 NEXT B
  80 NEXT A
  90 CLEAR #
     RUN
```

The author obtained the following results using a new cartridge.

```
10000000000000000000000000000000
00000000000000000000000000000000
00000000000000000000000000000000
00000000000000000000000000000000
00000000000000000000000110000000
00000000000000000000011111111111
11111111111111111111111111111111
11111111111111111111111111111111
```

The sector-bits are given in ascending numerical order — sector 0, sector 1, ..., sector 256 — although they are created in the opposite order (and occur on the tape in the opposite order).

In the above map sector 0 is non-existent; sectors 151 & 152 are unusable and presumably are the 'splice' region of the tape; and sectors 181-255 are non-existent. There are 178 sectors in working order and, indeed, **CAT** 1 & **ENTER** returned 89 K for the amount of room available to the user on this tape.

The following results were obtained after **SAVE**ing a 7½K BASIC program.

```
10000000000000000000000000000000
00000000000000000000000000000000
00000000000001010101010101010101
01010101010000000000000000000000
00000000000000000000000110000000
00000000000000000000011111111111
11111111111111111111111111111111
11111111111111111111111111111111
```

Note that the records are not in contiguous sectors — after creating a record there is insufficient time to 'fetch' a further 512 bytes of data into the channel area and still 'catch' the next sector.

Final note — IOBORD:

The 'shadow' system variable IOBORD, location 23750 dec. (5CC6h), normally holds '0'; and this leads to the border on the TV display to flash 'black' when blocks of data are transferred from the **Spectrum** to a **Microdrive** (but not vice versa). The user is able to alter the value in IOBORD — range 0-7 — and so change the colour of the border during the output operation.

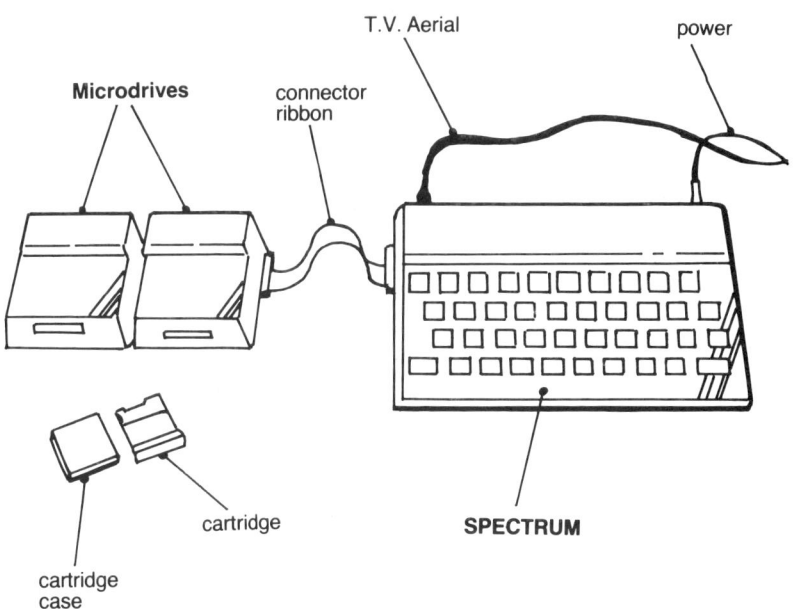

Photograph 1. The Extended **Spectrum** System (**ZX Interface 1** is not visible)

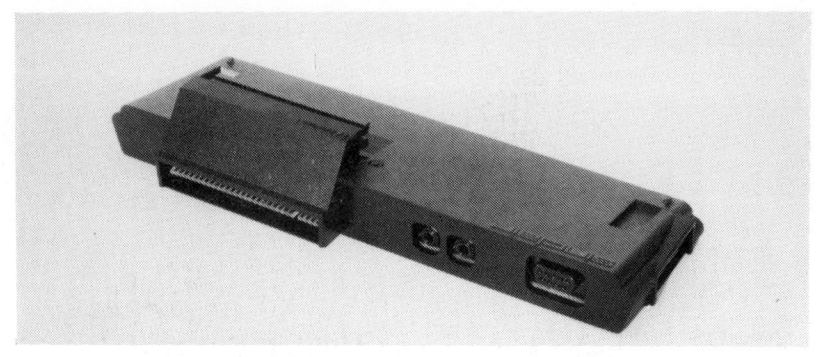

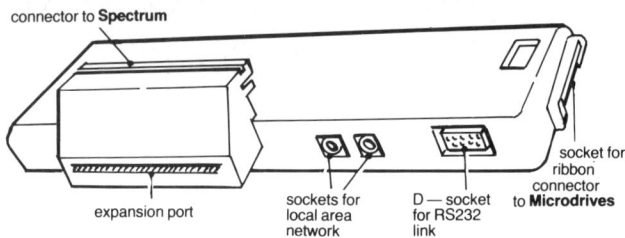

Photograph 2. The **ZX Interface 1** — seen from rear.

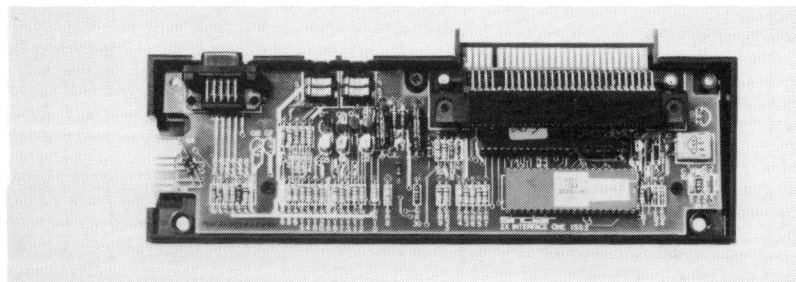

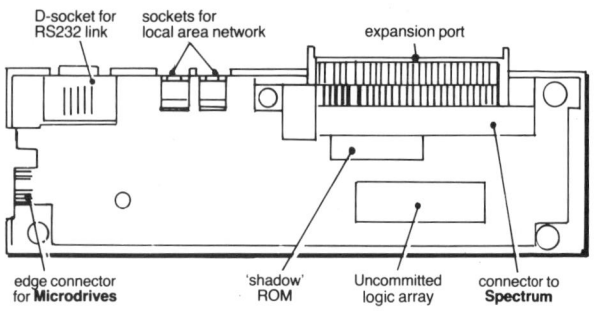

Photograph 3. The **ZX Interface 1** — internal view

Photograph 3. The **ZX Interface 1** — internal view

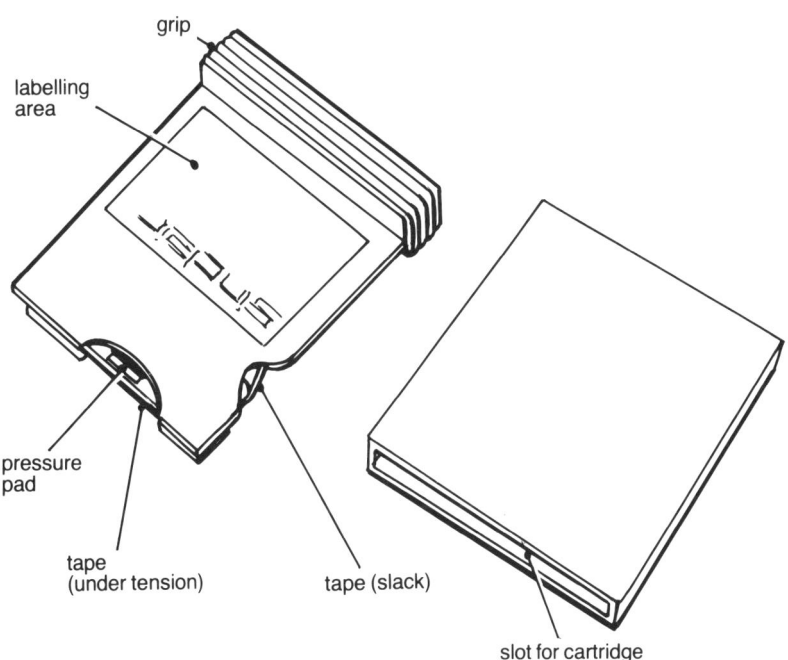

Photograph 4. A **Microdrive** cartridge and its case.

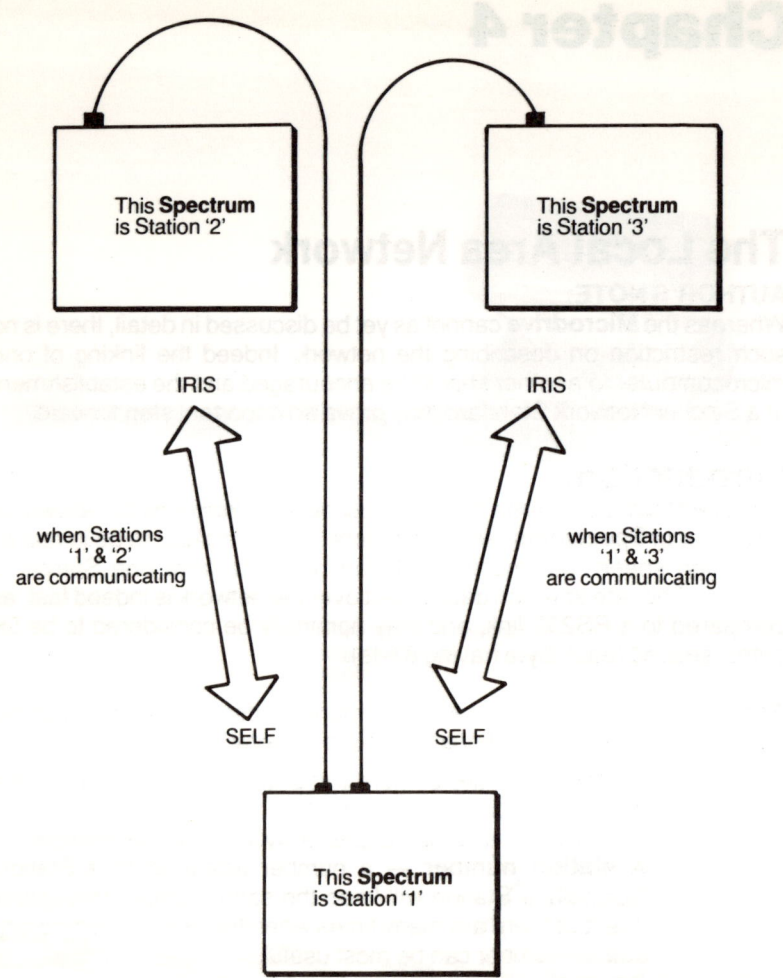

Note: The users of **Spectrums** '2' & '3' will each have their own views of this network.

Diagram 1. A Network with three Stations.

Diagram 1 shows a simple **Spectrum** network labelled to match the above definitions.

Using the network:
The operation of the **Spectrum** network will in most cases be performed using BASIC statements and the appropriate statements will now be discussed from the view of the user.

Changing a Station's number:
When the power is first connected to a **Spectrum** fitted with a **ZX Interface 1** the **Spectrum** does not have a station number; however when the 'shadow ROM' is 'paged in' for the first time then the Spectrum will be made Station '1'. This station number is held as the 'shadow' system variable NTSTAT, location 23749. Thereafter the user can change the station number of the SELF **Spectrum** by using:

either **FORMAT** "N", station number
or **POKE** 23749, station number

Station numbers normally have the range 1-64. (This restriction does not apply when using the network from machine code.)
The current station number of a **Spectrum** is copied into the channel area whenever a 'net channel' is created; and if the station number is changed subsequently then it is quite possible, and useful, to have 'net channels' with different station numbers for the receiving, or sending, of data files.

SAVEing a program, array or code block:
BASIC programs, named arrays and blocks of data can be sent to another Station — from SELF to IRIS — using a **SAVE** statement.
   e.g. **SAVE** *"n",2
   — where IRIS is station '2'.
   SAVE *"N";3 **LINE** 10
   — where IRIS is station '3' and the program is 'auto-run'.
   SAVE *"N";0 SCREEN$
   — where IRIS can be anyone who is awaiting a 'broadcast'.
In the examples above complete communication with the IRIS Station will only occur if IRIS is awaiting the communication. When IRIS is specified (other than zero) then IRIS must be waiting for a communication from SELF; and if the program is sent as a 'broadcast' then any Station wishing to be IRIS must be expecting a 'broadcast'.

Communication with a specified IRIS involves a strict protocol of 'acknowledgements'; whereas a 'broadcast' is not acknowledged and indeed can be 'received' by any number of Stations at the same time if more than one Station is ready for the 'broadcast'. A program sent as a 'broadcast' is handled at a much slower rate (about four times slower) than a program sent to a specific IRIS.

LOADing, MERGEing or VERIFYing a program, array or code block:

BASIC programs, named arrays and blocks of data can be received from another Station — from IRIS to SELF — using, as required and allowed, **LOAD**, **MERGE** & **VERIFY** statements.

    e.g. **LOAD** *"n";2 **DATA**
    — the 'source' is Station '2'.
    VERIFY *"n",0
    — the 'broadcast' is to be checked against the currently held BASIC program.
    MERGE *"N";1
    — the program received from Station '1' will be **MERGE**d with the currently held program. Note that it does not matter if SELF is also a Station '1'.

As with **SAVE**ing a BASIC program over the network it is essential that IRIS is prepared to send the expected material.

The protocol for passing a BASIC program, named array or block of code from one Station to another over the network is shown in diagram 2. However it is not possible in a diagram to show a 'waiting' computer. In the example if — **SAVE** *"N";2 — should be entered before — **LOAD** *"N";1 — Station '1' will 'wait' for Station '2' to be ready; and vice versa. Then, only when they are both 'ready' will the program be sent. The program is divided into 'buffers' of 255 bytes and whilst a Station is 'waiting', either initially or between 'buffers', the border of the T.V. screen will flash (as with **SAVE**ing and **LOAD**ing from cassette). The colour of the border will switch between its 'current' colour and the colour held by the 'shadow' system variable IOBORD, address 23750 (range of values 0-7). The user may change the value held in IOBORD as desired.

The using of a **SAVE**, **LOAD**, **VERIFY** or **MERGE** statement does not involve the opening or closing of streams. Instead a 'net channel' is created in the SELF **Spectrum** on an 'ad hoc' basis. (Ad hoc = for a particular purpose.) A 'net channel' created for this purpose is 'reclaimed' once it is no longer required.

Sending data over the network:

The three BASIC commands — **OPEN #**, **PRINT #** and **CLOSE #** — allow the user to send data over the network.

beforehand:
(a) Users agree to use station numbers '1' & '2'
(b) Users agree Station '1' will send its program to Station '2'

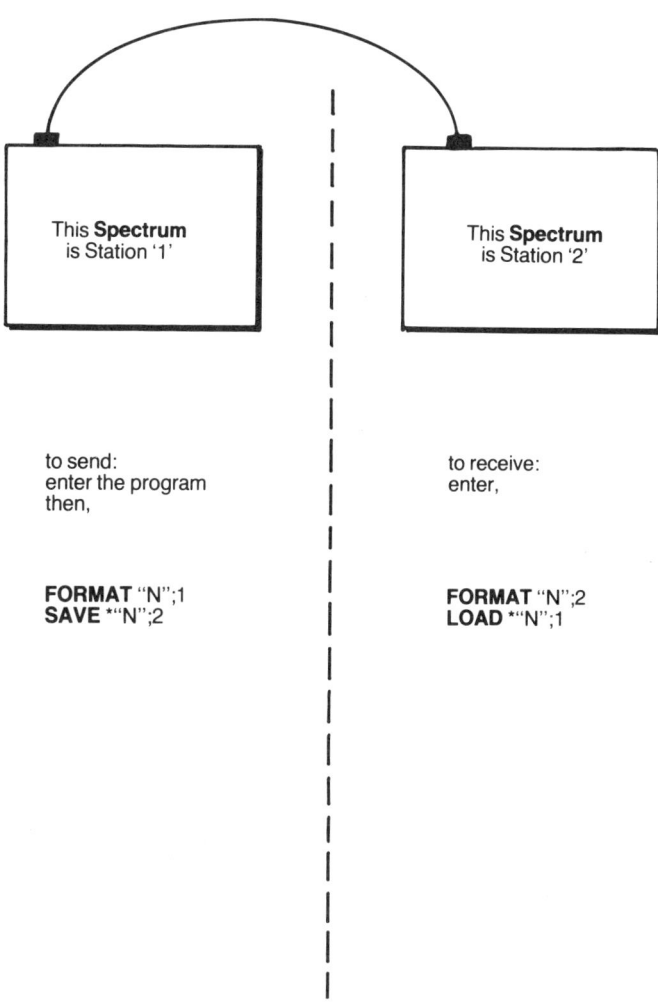

to send:
enter the program
then,

FORMAT "N";1
SAVE *"N";2

to receive:
enter,

FORMAT "N";2
LOAD *"N";1

afterwards
The identical program will be held in each **Spectrum**.

Diagram 2. Passing a BASIC program over the network

The data may be considered as either:

> a collection of 'printable expressions' and separated by 'carriage return' characters,

or:

> a collection of single characters.

The first stage involved in the sending of data is the creation of a 'net channel' for the purpose of communicating from SELF to IRIS. This is performed by using an **OPEN #** statement.

> e.g. **OPEN** #4;"N";18
> — associate stream '4' with a new 'net channel' for communication from SELF to IRIS, Station '18'.
> **OPEN** #5; "n",0
> — associate stream '5' with a new 'net channel' that will 'broadcast' data.

The detailed contents of a 'net channel' will be discussed later in this chapter; but a 'net channel' always contains a 'net buffer' of 255 locations. This means that up to 255 bytes of data can be collected before being sent to IRIS over the network.

The second stage involves the filling of the 'net buffer' with the necessary data. This is performed using a **PRINT #** command with the necessary stream number.

If the data is to be considered as 'expressions' (to be read using **INPUT**, see below) then care must be taken to ensure that the 'carriage return' characters are placed appropriately; i.e. as one presses **ENTER** after replying to an **INPUT** prompt.

Examples of sensible **PRINT #** statements are:

> **PRINT** #4;1
> — the characters that go into the 'buffer' are: '1' & 'carriage return'.
> **PRINT** #4;"ONE"
> — the characters that go into the 'buffer' are: 'O', 'N', 'E' & 'carriage return'.
> **PRINT** #4;A'B$
> — the characters that go into the 'buffer' are: the printed characters of the variable A, 'carriage return', the printed characters of the variable B$ & 'carriage return'.

A 'net buffer' can only hold 255 characters and when an attempt is made to 'buffer' a 256th character then this character is 'preserved' whilst the full 'buffer' is sent to IRIS. The 'preserved' character afterwards forms the first character of the next 'buffer'.

The third stage involves the closing down of the stream. The BASIC command **CLOSE #** first sends any partially filled 'net buffer' to IRIS, secondly 'reclaims' the 'net channel' and thirdly **CLOSE**s the stream by writing zeroes into the 'stream data bytes' (original values for streams 0-3).

    E.g. **CLOSE** #4
    — closes down the stream.

Receiving data over the network:
The four BASIC commands — **OPEN#**, **INPUT#**, **INKEY$#** and **CLOSE#** — allow the user to receive data over the network. As with the operation of sending data the 'data' may be considered as; 'expressions' and required to be separated by 'carriage return' characters; or as a collection of single characters.

Once again the first stage involves **OPEN**ing a stream.
E.g. **OPEN** #7;"N";1
— associate stream '7' with a new 'net channel' for communication from IRIS, station '1', to SELF.
OPEN #6,"n",0
— associate stream '6' with a new 'net channel' that will receive a 'broadcast'.

The second stage involves the use of **INPUT#** and **INKEY$#** commands. But note that it is inappropriate to read 'single character data' using **INPUT#**.

Examples of these commands are:
    INPUT #7;A
    — a set of 'received bytes', limited by a 'carriage return' character are assigned to the variable A. The 'expression' to be assigned must be numeric, i.e. would be accepted by —
    VAL " . . . expression . . . ".
    INPUT #7;A$
    — the 'expression' is considered as a string of characters (of finite length).
    INKEY$ #7
    — the string returned by this function will be the next 'received character'.

In all cases the 'net channel' is examined to determine whether there is any 'received data'; if not then a fresh 'buffer' is taken from IRIS. However if the 'last buffer' was marked 'end of file' then no request is made to IRIS and the error report 'end of file' is given.

There is a special feature about the use of **INKEY$#** when used with specific IRIS stations (not a 'broadcast' situation). **INKEY$#** is normally expected to return the 'next received byte' as a single character string; but it has been arranged that **INKEY$#** will return a 'null' string if IRIS is not awaiting a request from SELF to send another 'buffer'. This facility allows the user of SELF to **poll** Stations and collect data from any Station that is ready to send it.

The third stage involves closing down the stream by using a **CLOSE#** command. Any unused 'received data' is lost.

    E.g. **CLOSE** #7
    — 'reclaim' the 'net channel' and make the 'stream data bytes' zero.

The protocol for passing data over the network is shown in diagram 3. Once again it is not possible to show how the 'source' Station waits for the 'destination' Station to be ready; and vice versa.

The technical details of the Spectrum network:

The following details will be of interest to **Spectrum** owners who use the network from BASIC, as outlined above; but a clear idea of just how the network is managed is really only needed by users who wish to use, or modify, the network from machine code.

The network itself is a 2-wire system. One wire acts as a ground reference point — nominally 0v., and the other wire as a signal wire which is **active high**, nominally 5v., and **inactive low**, as ground.

At any instance in time the network can be considered as **resting**, unused; or **claimed**, in use. Although whilst **claimed** the network will frequently be **inactive** — but never for as long a period as if it were **resting**. It is always the 'source' computer that 'claims' the network; whilst the 'destination' computer has the minor role of 'reading' the network and then replying if required.

beforehand:
(a) Users agree to use station numbers '1' & '2'
(b) Users agree Station '1' will send a set of numbers to Station '2'

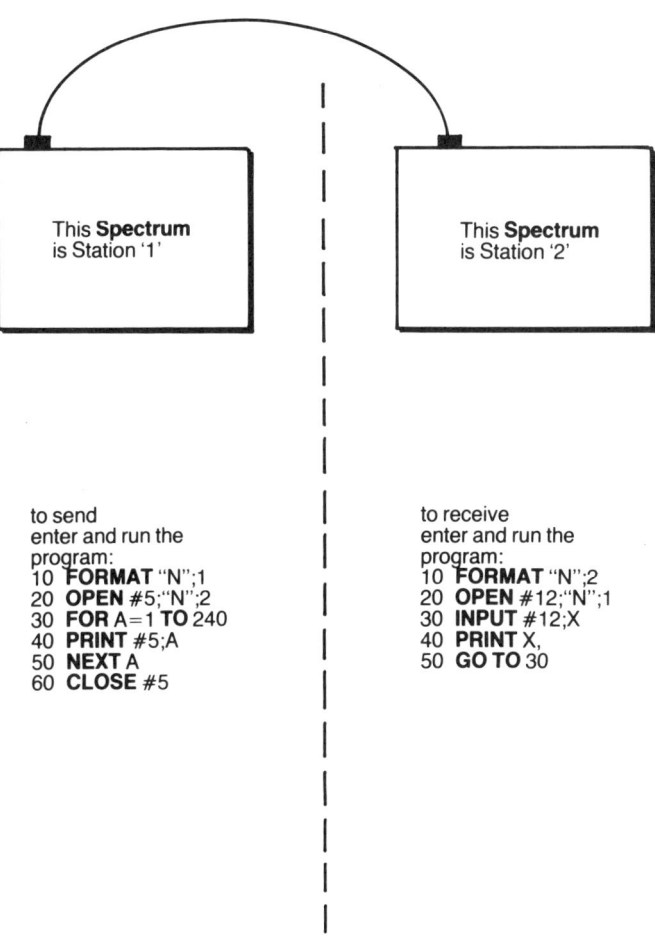

to send
enter and run the
program:
10 **FORMAT** "N";1
20 **OPEN** #5;"N";2
30 **FOR** A=1 **TO** 240
40 **PRINT** #5;A
50 **NEXT** A
60 **CLOSE** #5

to receive
enter and run the
program:
10 **FORMAT** "N";2
20 **OPEN** #12;"N";1
30 **INPUT** #12;X
40 **PRINT** X,
50 **GO TO** 30

Diagram 3. Passing data over the network — using **PRINT#** & **INPUT#**.

The protocol for communicating from one Station to another follows a strict format and in the discussion below the steps will be discussed initially from the view that the user's **Spectrum** SELF is sending one or more 'buffers' of data to the 'destination' Station IRIS. In the first instance no timing details will be given but they will be discussed at the end of the chapter.

Claiming the network:

This is the first stage in any communication. As the network may be either **resting** or **claimed** by another Station, the user's **Spectrum** SELF must examine the network repeatedly until it is satisfied the network is indeed **resting**. The time spent doing this 'examination' is a 'sufficient' time plus a 'randomised' extra amount. SELF now sends out, slowly, a 'leader' pulse and its 8-bit station number. The value sent is taken from NTSTAT and is the 'global' station number; this is not necessarily the same as the value held in NCSELF. The separate bits of the station number are sent 'inverted' with the most significant bit being sent first. Each bit **activates** the network only if it was originally a zero; and makes the network **inactive** if it was a '1'. Before handling another bit, a check is made to ensure that the network has the expected state from the present bit; and

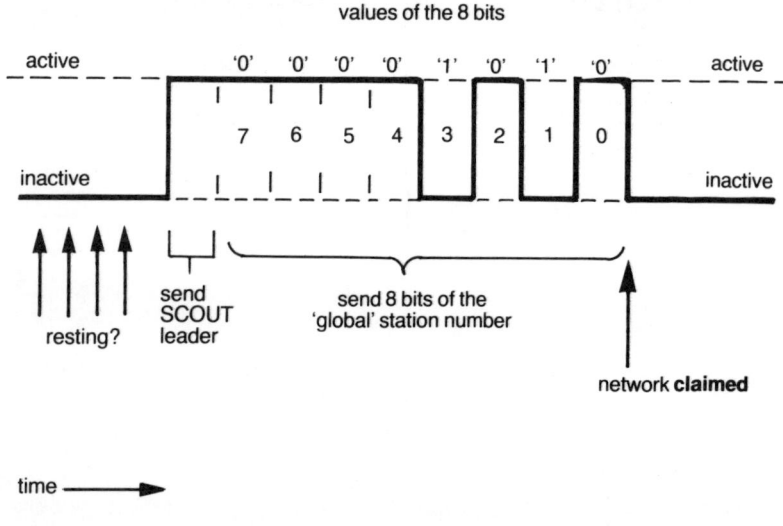

Diagram 4. Station '10' sending its SCOUT.

if the wrong state is found then the whole operation of claiming the network is started again. Once all the bits of the station number have been sent (and read-back successfully) the network can be considered to be **claimed**. The action of sending the station number forms a SCOUT: and all Stations that are listening to the network set their timings from when they first detect a SCOUT 'leader' pulse.

Diagram 4 shows the Station '10' claiming the network by sending its SCOUT.

Sending a HEADER:

Once the network has been claimed by the sending of a SCOUT, an 8-byte HEADER is sent. The data for the HEADER comes from the HEADER bytes of the net channel.

A net channel has the following structure:

bytes	contents	
0-1	Address 0008h	
2-3	Address 0008h	
4	"N"	("N" + 80h if 'ad hoc')
5-6	Address OUT_N	(output address)
7-8	Address IN_N	(input address)
9-10	Number 0114h	(276 dec. bytes in a net channel)

; the following eight locations hold the HEADER bytes

11	NCIRIS	(the IRIS Station number i.e. the 'other' Station)
12	NCSELF	(own Station number, same as NTSTAT when channel created)
13-14	NCNUMB	(block number, range 0-65535)
15	NCTYPE	(ordinarily '0' — for data but '1' for 'end of file')
16	NCOBL	(output buffer length, range 0-255; will be '0' when buffer is used for 'receiving')
17	NCDCS	(8-bit checksum for data)
18	NCHCS	(8-bit checksum for preceding seven bytes)

;the next two locations are used during 'receiving'

19	NCCUR	(position of last character taken from buffer)
20	NCIBL	(the number of bytes that may be read from the data buffer)

;the data buffer is used for either 'receiving' or 'sending'

21-275	NCB	(255 byte data buffer)

The HEADER bytes describe the 'data block' that will be sent later. The 'data block' will be a copy of the present buffer.

The HEADER bytes are sent by calling the OUTPAK subroutine in the 'shadow' ROM. The E register will hold the value 08h and the HL register pair the address of NCIRIS.

The OUTPAK sends out bytes of data as follows:

- an initial **active** leader

then for each byte:

- an **inactive** starting period
- an **inactive/active** period for each **reset/set** bit; the least significant bit is handled first.
- an **active** stop period

finally:

- the network is made **inactive**

Diagram 5 shows the steps.

Following the sending of the HEADER bytes the value of NCIRIS is examined and if it is other than '0' then a 'response' is awaited from IRIS. A '0' would indicate a 'broadcast' which is never acknowledged.

A 'response' is a single byte of data and it is handled by IRIS using its OUTPAK subroutine. The SELF **Spectrum** accepts the 'response' as YES if a byte of value '1' is received from IRIS without undue delay.

The INPAK subroutine is used to collect the 'response'. On entry to this subroutine the E register holds the value 01h and the HL register pair the address of the 'shadow' system variable NTRESP, address 23757.

If there is not a correct 'response' received before 'time-out' then the whole operation of claiming the network, sending a SCOUT, sending a HEADER and awaiting a 'response' is repeated. To the user this situation is signalled by the colour of the border remaining a single colour — the IOBORD colour. However when the INPAK subroutine returns a byte and it is found to be a '1', then the 'data block' can be sent.

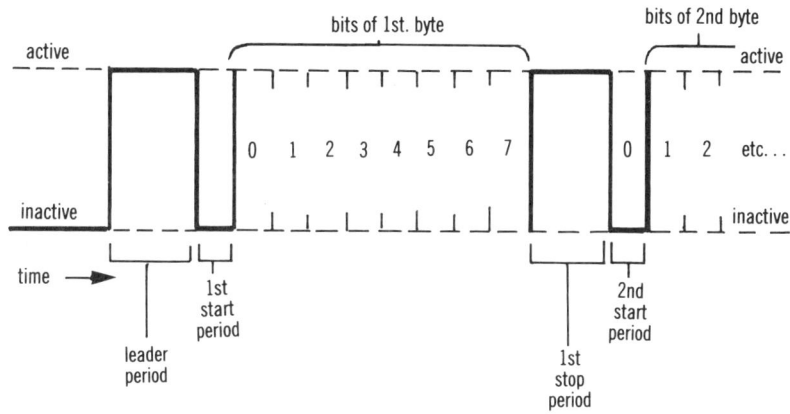

Diagram 5. Bytes of data being sent by the OUTPAK subroutine

Sending a data block:
The present 'buffer' of characters is sent by once again calling the OUTPAK subroutine. On this occasion the E register holds the current length of the 'buffer' — copied from NCOBL, and the HL register pair holds the address of the first 'buffer' byte — the address NCB.

Once the 'data block' has been sent the NCIRIS variable is examined again and a 'response' is awaited unless the 'data block' formed part of a 'broadcast'. As before if there is not a correct 'response' received before 'time-out' then the whole operation has to be repeated from claiming the network afresh.

Block numbers:
The 'data blocks' are considered as being numbered, from 0-65535. The creation of a 'net channel' makes the first block 'number 0' and subsequent 'data blocks' are numbered in order. The operation of sending a set of 'data blocks', as would be involved in the sending of a long BASIC program over the network, therefore involves the sending of block 'number 0', block 'number 1', ..., block 'number n'; where 'n' is the number of the 'end of file' block.

The steps involved in receiving one or more 'data blocks' will now be discussed.

Identifying a SCOUT:
The first stage in establishing communication from IRIS to SELF is the identification of a SCOUT (not necessarily from IRIS). A SCOUT can be found by finding the network becoming **active** after a **resting** period. This stage therefore involves SELF repeatedly examining the network until it is satisfied that the network is **resting** (taking 'sufficient' time without any extra amount, see earlier) and then waiting for the network to become **active**. This point corresponds to IRIS sending the 'leader' to its SCOUT — this always **activates** the network. The actual station number that IRIS is sending as a SCOUT is not required by SELF, so after identifying the start of the SCOUT the SELF computer simply waits until the network becomes **inactive** following the 8-bits of the station number.

It is intended that any **Spectrum** 'listening' to the network will always find the 'claiming' SCOUT.

Receiving a HEADER:
The IRIS computer sends an 8-byte HEADER shortly after its SCOUT has **claimed** the network, and the SELF computer 'reads' the eight bytes using the INPAK subroutine. The bytes are loaded into the 'shadow' system variables NTDEST — NTHCS, addresses 23758-23765. Diagram 6 shows the details involved in the reading of bytes from the network. The most important point to be made is that the 'period of uncertainty' is minimised by using electronic circuitry in the **ZX Interface 1** to synchronise the reading of the bits to their 'mid-cycle' points.

Examining the HEADER:
Once received, the HEADER has to be examined in order to decide whether or not to accept the 'data block' that is expected to follow it.

The steps involved are posed as a series of questions and in all cases a false answer leads to the SCOUT, HEADER & data block being 'passed over' and the next SCOUT sought.

- were eight bytes actually found?
- does the sum of the first seven bytes give the same value as the eighth byte, i.e. is NTHCS, the HEADER checksum, correct?
- is the block number as found in NTNUMB the expected block number?
  — Should it be the previous block number then IRIS is trying to repeat a block that SELF has already received but the 'response' was lost. In this case the block will be 'accepted' but 'passed over'.

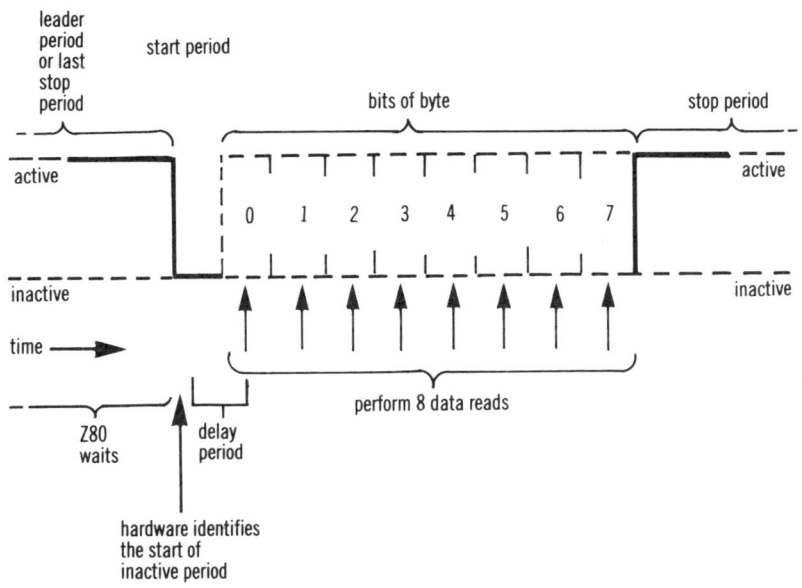

Diagram 6. Bytes of data being received by the INPAK subroutine.

- If a 'broadcast' is sought, is the HEADER part of a 'broadcast', i.e. are NTDEST & NCIRIS both zero? Otherwise, with a specified IRIS Station, does the HEADER say the 'data block' is for SELF, i.e. are NTDEST & NCSELF equal?
and
Is the IRIS Station using the required station number, i.e. are NTSRCE & NCIRIS equal?

Once the HEADER has been accepted the 'response', a byte of value '1', is sent using the OUTPAK subroutine. Remember that if a 'broadcast' is accepted then no 'response' will be sent.

Receiving a data block:

As long as the IRIS station does receive the 'response' from SELF before 'time-out', if not handling a 'broadcast', then IRIS will send a 'data block'.

The SELF computer receives this 'data block' by loading the value found in NTLEN — the length of the 'data block' — into the E register, the address NCB — the base address of the data buffer of the current 'net channel' — into the HL register pair and calling the INPAK subroutine.

Once received, the sum of the bytes in the new 'buffer' is compared against its checksum — found in NTDCS, and the 'response' sent if the numbers do match. If the checksum fails then the IRIS station will start afresh with an attempt to send the data; whilst SELF tries again to read it.

If all has gone without any problems the 'data buffer' of the 'net channel' will now contain up to '255' fresh bytes of data.

Further points:
Competition between Spectrums trying to claim the network:
It is intended that there should be minimal contention between **Spectrums** when more than one machine is trying to **claim** the network at the same time. The use of the 'extra' randomised time when trying to find the network **resting**, and the sending of the 'global' station number as a SCOUT, both help to resolve contention. Indeed if two or more **Spectrums** start sending out SCOUTS simultaneously (hopefully itself unlikely) then the Station sending the lower valued station number should **claim** the network successfully in all cases; the other **Spectrums** backing off and trying again later. The users can help with the last point by using different 'global' station numbers whenever possible.

Confusion when receiving 'broadcasts':
It is possible that if more than one Station are sending 'broadcasts' at the same time that the receiving Station may on occasions take one 'data block' from one machine and the next block from another. This occurs as the blocks that form a 'broadcast' are sent with large delays between them — so as to ensure that the 'recipient' has sufficient time to handle the data no matter what other work needs to be done; whilst the 'recipient' will overall spend a lot of time listening to the network.

This problem can only be overcome by the users taking care when sending a lot of 'broadcast' material.

Time-out using INKEY$
A station that is listening to the network in consequence of a **LOAD, VERIFY, MERGE** or **INPUT** command, will 'wait' indefinitely if the correct SCOUT, HEADER & 'data block' fail to appear on the network and are interpreted correctly. However when a byte of data is required in consequence of an **INKEY$#** command the the Station will only wait until 'time-out' before returning a 'null' string.

End of file details — sending data:
As new bytes of data are added to the buffer of the 'net channel' a record of the 'length' of the buffer is kept in the variable NCOBL and the value in NCTYPE will always be zero. Then, when an attempt is made to enter a

256th. byte the present buffer will be sent as a 'data block' containing 255 bytes of **ordinary data**. However if the last of a set of data bytes has been entered into the buffer then NCTYPE will be given the value '1' and the buffer sent as a 'data block' of up to 255 bytes of **closing data**.

This operation of making a 'data block' the 'end of file' block only occurs with:

- completion of the **SAVE** operation.
- closing the stream using **CLOSE #**.

End of file details — receiving data
As bytes of data are read from the buffer of a 'net channel' the value of the variable NCCUR is increased until the point is reached when there are no bytes left unused. Normally following a request for another character a fresh 'data block' would be sought but this only occurs if the current value of NTTYPE is '0'. If NTTYPE holds '1' then the 'end of file' has been found and the appropriate error message is produced.

Timing details with respect to the network:
A **Spectrum** has a clock rate of 3.5 mHz. and in the following discussion the timing details wil be given in T cycles where each cycle takes 1/3,500,000 of a second.

Sending data:
The network is considered to be **resting** if it is **inactive** for approximately 10,500 T cycles (3 ms.).

The SCOUT leader starts 22 T cycles after the last examination of the network and lasts for 181 T cycles. The 8-bits of the station number also last for 181 T cycles each. The pulses are 'read-back' after 136 T cycles.

The network is now **claimed** and the leader to the 8-bytes of the HEADER follows after a further 271 T cycles.

The HEADER bytes are sent using the OUTPAK subroutine and the format is always the same:

> leader period — 98 T cycles

then for each byte:

> a start period of 40 T cycles
> 8-bits each of 40 T cycles
> a stop period of 145 T cycles (but the final stop period is 86 T cycles).

The 'data block' will follow the HEADER after approximately 600 T cycles in the case of a 'broadcast', but delayed for up to 9000 T cycles if a 'response' is to be found and examined.

The duration of the 'data block' will be from 544 T cycles — one byte, to approximately 128,000 T cycles (37 ms.) — 255 bytes.

Diagram 7 shows these timings.

Receiving data:

Of necessity the receiving of data complements the sending of data but the following points can usefully be made.

The network is examined repeatedly over a period of approximately 7000 T cycles (2 ms.) to prove that the network is indeed **resting**.

Thereafter the network is examined once every 55 T cycles until it is found **active**. This should lead to a SCOUT being identified within the first third of the SCOUT's leader period. The actual details of the SCOUT are not required so the **Spectrum** wastes time until the SCOUT is finished.

A call is made to the INPAK subroutine to collect the 8 bytes of the HEADER that will come next. This subroutine is entered during the **inactive** period (271 T cycles) that separates the SCOUT and the HEADER.

The network is then examined every 35 T cycles in order to identify the presence of the leader period. Thereafter the synchronising hardware of the **ZX Interface 1** identifies the falling edge at the beginning of a start period. There will always be a 'degree of uncertainty' in finding the onset of the start period but the use of hardware to perform this task reduces the uncertainty considerably.

The rest of the start period is 'passed over' and the 8 bits of the byte are then collected at the rate of 1 bit every 40 T cycles. Again there will be a 'degree of uncertainty' involved in this progress as the clock of the **Spectrum** producing the signals may be running at a slightly different speed as compared to the clock in the receiving **Spectrum**. The system of synchronising on the start period allows for a difference of about 5 per cent between clock speeds.

Once the bytes of the HEADER have been obtained, they must be examined. If a 'broadcast' is being handled then no 'response' is to be sent and the **Spectrum** must be ready to find the leader to the 'data

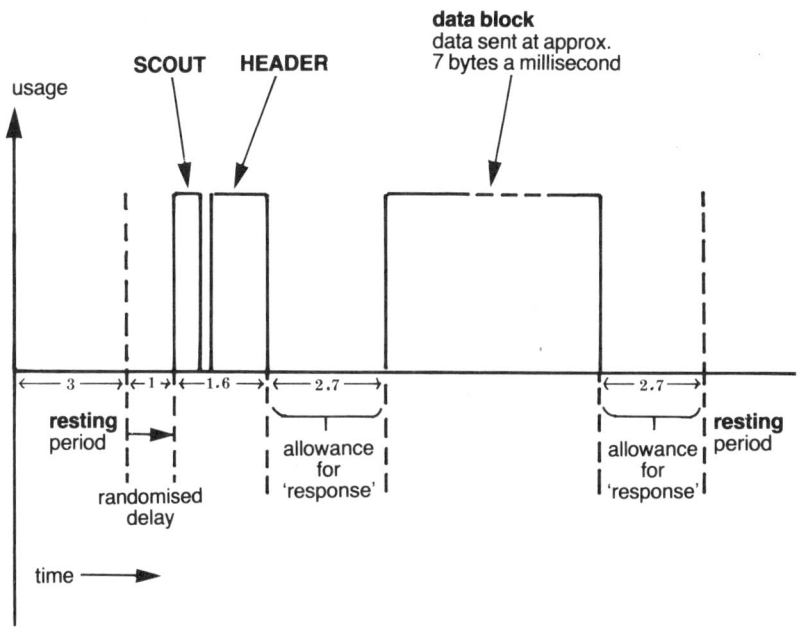

Diagram 7. Timing diagram for 'sending' over the network.

block' within 600 T cycles of the end of the HEADER bytes. However if the 'sending' **Spectrum** is expecting a 'response' then this must be sent within approximately 9000 T cycles.

The 'data block' is collected by calling the INPAK subroutine a second time; and again the 'receiving' **Spectrum** has 9000 T cycles in which to send its 'response'.

Chapter 5

The RS232 Link

Introduction
The third facility offered by the **ZX Interface 1** is the RS232 link.

The two principle uses of the RS232 link are expected to be:

— linking a **Spectrum** to a printer (other than the ZX printer)
— linking a **Spectrum** to another computer (possibly another **Spectrum** — an alternative to using the Local Area Network).

But the link can be used between a **Spectrum** and any other RS232 compatible device.

Using the RS232 link:
The rate at which data is transferred between devices joined by an RS232 link is termed the 'baud rate'; and upon initialisation the **ZX Interface 1** gives a default rate of '9600'.

Note: The theoretical rate at which bytes of data are transferred is given by:

baud rate/11   **bytes per second.**

However a byte of data is only transmitted when the receiving device signals that is indeed ready to accept the byte of data and there must be gaps between bytes; so the actual rate at which bytes are transferred is usually considerably less than that implied by the baud rate.

Setting the baud rate:
The baud rate will normally be set by using a **FORMAT** statement;

e.g. **FORMAT** "b";110

and the following rates are permitted;

50, 110, 300, 600, 1200, 2400, 4800, 9600, 19200.

Note that the lowest rate is '50' and the highest '19200' and if a number outside this range is used in a **FORMAT** statement then the baud rate will be set to its limit value as appropriate.

e.g. **FORMAT** "b";0 — sets the baud rate to '50'.

Also, if a **FORMAT** statement gives an intermediate value then the discrete baud rate below that value is used instead.

e.g. **FORMAT** "b";1500 — sets the baud rate to '1200'.

The only effect of a **FORMAT** is to set the values in the two bytes of the system variable BAUD and it is therefore possible to set the baud rate by using **POKE** statements or machine code 'LD' instructions if the user so wishes. In such a case the value for BAUD is given by:

(3500000/(26*baud rate)) −2

and it is possible to set the baud rate to either a standard or a non-standard rate.

SAVEing a program, array or code block:
BASIC programs, named arrays and blocks of data can be sent over the RS232 link by using the **SAVE** command. E.g.

SAVE *"b"
— a copy of the presently held program and its current variable are sent.
SAVE *"b" **SCREEN$**
— a copy of the current display and attributes file is sent.

LOADing, MERGEing or VERIFYing a program, array or code block:
BASIC programs, named arrays and blocks of data can be received over the RS232 link. E.g.

LOAD *"b"
— a BASIC program and its variables will be **LOAD**ed.
MERGE *"b"
— a BASIC program and its variables will be **MERGE**d.

VERIFY *"b" DATA 32000,100
— a block of data will be **VERIFY**ed against the present contents of the RAM.

In all the cases using **SAVE, LOAD, MERGE** or **VERIFY** the device expression "b" or "B" must be used as the full range of values, 0-255 decimal, must be allowed for each byte.

Also note that the data will only be transferred over the RS232 link if the 'receiver' signals to the 'sender' that the device is 'ready'. As with the network the border colour of the screen during data transfers and waiting periods is specified by the value held in the system variable IOBORD and can be changed by the user as required.

Sending data over the RS232 link:

As with the Local Area Network, the sending of data involves the **OPEN**ing of a stream to be associated with the RS232 link before a **PRINT** statement is used. E.g.

OPEN #4;"b"
— stream '4' is **OPEN**ed for use with the RS232 link.

A stream **OPEN**ed in this manner can now be used for either the sending or receiving of bytes of data. This is possible as there is no 'buffer' system and each byte is handled in turn.

The action of **OPEN**ing a stream for RS232 communication has the effect of adding '11' bytes of data to the channel information area. These bytes are:

bytes	contents	
1-2	Address 0008h.	
3-4	Address 0008h.	
5	"T"	("T" + 80h if 'ad hoc')
6-7	Address OUT_T2	(output address)
8-9	Address IN_T2	(input address)
10-11	Number '11'.	(eleven bytes in channel)

The 'shadow' ROM routines IN_T2 and OUT_T2 are the actual routines for handling the 'receiving' or 'sending' of a byte of data via the RS232 link.

Once a stream has been **OPEN**ed for RS232 communication the following commands can be used to handle information;

Sending:

>   **PRINT** #4;A
>   — the current 'printed' value of the variable 'A' will be 'sent'; followed by a 'carriage return'.
>   **PRINT** #4;"String of characters"
>   — the characters of the string will be sent; followed by a 'carriage return'.

Receiving:

>   **INPUT** #4;A$
>   — the set of characters received before a 'carriage return' will be assigned to A$.
>   **LET** A$=**INKEY$**#4
>   — the 'next' character will be assigned to A$. Note that **CODE** A$ will be zero if the user's **Spectrum** is not 'being sent' a character.

A **CLOSE** statement, e.g. **CLOSE** #4 will lead to an additional 'line feed' character, 0Ah, being sent before the '11' bytes of the RS232 channel are reclaimed.

Note that if the extra 'line feed' character proves a nuisance then its best to avoid **CLOSE**ing RS232 streams — using instead **CLEAR** # or an 'error situation' to reclaim the channel

The "T" system:

The device expressions "t" and "T" also enable the RS232 link. These expressions allow for an ASCII character and Sinclair token 'text mode'. The reason for this mode is that it allows for the command **LIST** #n, where n is an **OPEN**ed RS232 stream.

A **LIST**ing would be produced by, for example:

>   **OPEN** #4;"T"
>   **LIST** #4
>   **CLOSE** #4   — and the 'line feed' will probably be required.

In this 'text mode' the character codes are modified as follows:

- control codes (00h-1Fh) are ignored — except for 'carriage return' (0Dh) which is modified to give 'carriage return' and 'line feed' (0Dh & 0Ah),
- graphic codes are changed to '?' (3Fh),
- Sinclair tokens are expanded recursively.

Extended use of the "T" system:

It is possible for the user to join the **Spectrum** to an RS232 compatible printer and **PRINT** using any one of the three following methods:

1. use only a "B" stream - thereby allowing for the full range of bytes 00h-FFh. This method leaves the user with the task of handling control codes, graphic characters and tokens; but there are no limitations as to what can be done.

2. Using both a "T" stream and a "B" stream. When using this method the user can allow 'printable characters' to be handled by the "T" stream; and supplement the RS232 output by including "B" stream characters as requied.

    E.g. To send a printer 'escape' codes one might use:
    10 **OPEN** #4;"T": **OPEN** #5;"B" — "T" & "B" streams
    20 **PRINT** #5;**CHR$** 27;**CODE** "K"; — Escape "K"
    30 **PRINT** #4;"Print this now"

3. Using an extended "T" stream.
    As is mentioned above, a "T" stream will ignore all the codes 00h-1Fh (with the exception of 0Dh — 'carriage return'). This results in the user being unable to include the 'positional' controllers ',', '**AT**' and '**TAB**' in **PRINT** statements associated with a RS232 "T" stream. (Indeed spurious characters will be created if **AT** & **TAB** are followed by high parameter value.)

    The following BASIC program shows how the "T" stream can be ammended to cater for these 'positional' controllers if the user wishes to include them in **PRINT** statements.

Notes:
Line 10 — Stream '2' is being used; a machine code routine is located at 65000-65184; and a BASIC loader in lines 9800-9993.

Line 9830 — The 'column' number can be altered as required — here it is set to '40' columns. The current 'tab' position can be found by **PEEK**ing location 23728.

Line 9990 — The 'tab' position is incremented with every character that is printed; until the 'column' value resets the 'tab' position to zero as a line is filled.

Line 9991 — A 'carriage return' character also resets the 'tab' position.

Line 9992 — Deals with '**PRINT** comma'. The 'comma-tab' positions in this program are '0', '8', '16', '24' and '32'; and the incrementing value of '8' (second '8' in this line) can be altered if required. The **PRINT**ing of a comma will always advance the 'tab' position a minimum of one column.

Line 9993 — This line deals with **AT** and **TAB**. The column values of these controllers are taken 'modulo' the column width as specified in location 23729. All the colour item controllers are ignored correctly.

Note: The effect of **PRINT**ing with this program is to re-direct the output that normally goes to the upper part of the T.V. display, to the RS232 device.

```
  10 OPEN #2;"t": CLEAR 65499: GO SUB 9800
  20 REM . . . your printing . . .
  30 STOP
9800 REM #2 , AT TAB subroutine
9810 REM uses z,z1,z2,z3
9820 REM set tab and col values
9830 POKE 23728,0: POKE 23729,40
9840 REM look at stream #2
9850 LET z1=PEEK 23578+256*PEEK 23579
9860 IF NOT z1 THEN POKE 23610,23: STOP
9870 REM look at T channel
9880 LET z2=z1+PEEK 23631+256*PEEK 23632+3
9890 IF PEEK z2< >CODE "T" THEN POKE 23610,23: STOP
9900 REM alter output address
9910 POKE z2+1,232
9920 POKE z2+2,253
9930 REM enter machine code
9940 FOR z=0 TO 184
9950 READ z3
9960 POKE 65000+z,z3
```

9970 NEXT z
9980 RETURN
9990 DATA 254, 165, 48, 45, 33, 59, 92, 203, 134, 254, 32, 32, 2, 203, 198, 56, 22, 245, 253, 52, 118, 253, 126, 119, 253, 190, 118, 48, 7, 205, 19, 254, 253, 54, 118, 1, 241, 24, 10
9991 DATA 254, 13, 32, 9, 175, 50, 176, 92, 62, 13, 195, 60, 12
9992 DATA 254, 6, 32, 31, 237, 75, 176, 92, 30, 0, 12, 28, 121, 184, 40, 8, 214, 8, 40, 4, 48, 250, 24, 242, 213, 62, 32, 205, 232, 253, 209, 29, 200, 24, 245
9993 DATA 254, 22, 40, 12, 254, 23, 40, 8, 254, 16, 216, 17, 106, 254, 24, 3, 17, 98, 254, 50, 14, 92, 42, 81, 92, 213, 17, 5, 0, 25, 209, 115, 35, 114, 201, 17, 106, 254, 50, 15, 92, 24, 235, 17, 232, 253, 205, 85, 254, 87, 58, 14, 92, 254, 22, 40, 8, 254, 23, 63, 192, 58, 15, 92, 87, 58, 177, 92, 186, 40, 2, 48, 6, 71, 122, 144, 87, 24, 242, 58, 176, 92, 186, 200, 253, 190, 119, 162, 200, 62, 32, 213, 205, 232, 253, 209, 24, 237

The technical details of the RS232 link:
The RS232 link of the **ZX Interface 1** provides for both the 'sending' and 'receiving' of serial data between the user's **Spectrum** and a second device (possibly also a **Spectrum**).

The passing of data over a RS232 link is handled byte by byte and a byte of data will be transmitted only if the receiving device has signalled that it is indeed ready to receive.

The RS232 link is a 6-wire system. Two wires are used during 'sending', two during 'receiving', the fifth wire is a grounding wire and the sixth wire carrying a nominal 9v (not normally used).

The protocol for 'sending':
The wire along which the bytes of data are sent is called **RXdata** (short for 'received data line') and the level of the signal on this wire is set by the 'sending' device. The second wire involved in 'sending' is called **DTR** (short for 'data terminal ready') and this is set by the 'receiving' device.

The operation of sending a byte of data involves the following steps:

i. Wait until the line **DTR** becomes high.
ii. Send the byte of data.

The two steps then have to be repeated for every subsequent byte of data.

It is usual for the 'receiving' device to lower the signal level on the **DTR** once it has received a byte of data, so as to prevent the 'sender' from passing a further byte before the 'receiver' is ready for it (but see later).

The format of the **RXdata** signal is shown in diagram 1.

Note that '11' bits are sent in total for each byte of data:

— a start bit
— the eight data bits
— two stop bits (may be considered as a double length stop bit)

and that there is no parity bit.

The protocol for 'receiving':
The wire along which the bytes of data are received is called **TXdata** (short for 'transmitted data line') and the level of the signal is set by the

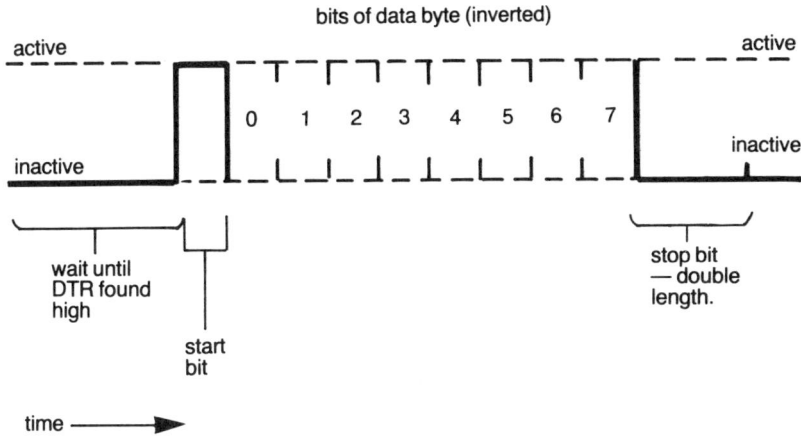

Note: length of bit = 47 + 26*BAUD T states.

Diagram 1. A byte of data being 'sent' via the RS232 link.

'sending' device. The second wire involved in 'receiving' is called **CTS** (short for 'clear to send line') and this is set by the 'receiving' device.

It follows that if two **Spectrums** are linked together by the RS232 system that **RXdata, DTR, TXdata & CTS** of one **Spectrum** will be connected to **TXdata, CTS, RXdata & DTR**, respectively, of the second **Spectrum**.

The operation of receiving a byte of data involves the following steps:

i. First examine the value in the 'shadow' system variable SER_FL (serial flat). If the value in the low byte is other than zero:—
THEN take the value in the high byte to be the required byte (it had been found earlier — see below); make the low byte of SER_FL zero before returning. **ELSE** proceed to 'receive' one, or two, bytes of data.
ii. Make the **CTS** line have a high signal level.
iii. Wait for the signal on **TXdata** to go high — this will be the beginning of the 'start bit'.

iv. Read the eight bits of the byte.
v. Save the complete byte.
vi. Make the **CTS** line have a low signal level.

Note: Although the **CTS** is now low it is possible that the 'sending' device may still send a further byte of data — this does not occur when a **Spectrum** is 'sending'.

vii. Repeat steps iii. & iv. if a second byte is being sent. This second byte goes into the second location of the system variable SER_FL; and the first location is set to the value '1'.

However if there is no further byte found within a given period of time, it is assumed that there is no second byte to be considered; SER_FL's low byte stays holding zero.

viii. The byte saved in step v. is retrieved and is taken to be the required byte.

Timing details with respect to the RS232 link:

The duration of each data bit sent over the RS232 link is given by:

$$\text{length of bit} = 47 + 26 * \text{BAUD T states.}$$

where a single T state is a 3,500,000th of a second.

The value of BAUD is given by:

$$\text{BAUD} = (3500000 / (\text{baud rate} * 26)) - 2$$

If the baud rate '19200' is considered then the length of each bit should theoretically be:

$$= 3500000/19200$$
$$= 182.3 \text{ t states}$$

Whereas, the actual rate is:

$$\text{BAUD} = \text{INT}(3500000/(19200*26)) - 2$$
$$= 7$$

and the length of a bit is:

$$= 47 + 26 * \text{BAUD}$$
$$= 177 \text{ T states}$$

I.e. At a baud rate of '19200' the error is less than 3%; and, at slower rates the 'error' will be much less.

Linking 'other' computers to the Spectrum system:

The **Spectrum**'s RS232 link allows for communication between the **Spectrum** and any other RS232 compatible computer. This means that other computers can use the **Microdrive**, the local area network and the ZX printer by treating the **Spectrum** as a 'controller'. It is probably possible to make a 'specific' interface between an 'other' computer and, for example, a Sinclair **Microdrive**; but it is likely that it will be cheaper and easier to use a **Spectrum** instead.

The following discussion describes how, in outline, an Acorn BBC microcomputer can be linked to a **Spectrum** system.

The BBC microcomputer has a RS423 5-pin socket that is directly compatible with the **Spectrum**'s RS232 connector. For communication in both directions the user has to connect the TXdata, RXdata, DTR, CTS & GND of the **Spectrum** to the data out, data in, RTS, CTS & GND of the BBC microcomputer, respectively. The baud rate will be '9600' by default on both machines.

Using the ZX printer:

The easiest example to consider first is the use of the ZX printer to print under the direction of the BBC microcomputer.

In the **Spectrum** the program is simply:

   MOVE "b" **TO** #3   &   **ENTER**

Of course, after connecting the ZX printer and the RS232 link connector.

In the BBC microcomputer the user enters — for DIRECT printing:

*FX5,2	— select serial device
CTRL B	— to 'turn on' the printer
......	
......	— All printing goes to the ZX printer
CTRL C	— to 'turn off' the printer

Or, in a program, perhaps:

```
10  *FX5,2        — select serial
20  VDU2          — = CTRL B
30  *FX21,2       — discards any characters in the
                    RS423 buffer
......
......            — The printing (use *FX3,7 if the
......              output to the screen is not required)
100 VDU3          — = CTRL C
```

Using the Microdrive:

The examples in this section show how the BBC microcomputer can use the **Microdrive** to store a 'data file'.
Note: It is possible to handle BASIC programs — treating them as a collection of 'data-bytes'; but the author does not know how to **SAVE** and **LOAD** via the RS423 interface of the BBC microcomputer — presumably it can be done using assembly language routines.

Creating a Microdrive file:

In the BBC microcomputer enter:

```
10  DIMA$(2)              ;create some data
20  LETA$(0)="aaaa"
30  LETA$(1)="bbbb"
40  LETA$(2)="cccc"
50  *FX5,2                ;select serial printer
60  VDU2                  ;prepare to send
70  PRINT 3               ;three items of data to form
                          ;the file
80  PRINTA$(0)            ;send the data
90  PRINTA$(1)
100 PRINTA$(2)
110 VDU3                  ;stop sending
```

Whilst, on the **Spectrum** use:

```
10  OPEN #4;"b"                ;read on stream '4'
20  OPEN #5;"M";1;"BBC1"       ;store on stream '5'
30  INPUT #4;A                 ;fetch 'number'
40  FOR N=1 TO A
50  INPUT #4;A$                ;fetch each data-item
60  PRINT #5;A$                ;send it to Microdrive buffer
70  NEXT N                     ;
80  CLOSE #4                   ;close the input stream
90  CLOSE #5                   ;create the Microdrive file
                               ;and reclaim the channel
```

It is, of course, possible to have the BBC microcomputer send the name of the file-to-be; and for the **Spectrum** to create such a file with the first data-item in the file being the 'length' of the file.

Reading a Microdrive file:
The reverse operation might be (knowing that file "BBC1" has three string data-items):

In the **Spectrum** enter:

```
10 OPEN #5;"M";1;"BBC1"    ;read on stream '5'
20 OPEN #4;"b"             ;send on stream '4'
30 FOR N=1 TO 3
40 INPUT #5;A$             ;fetch each data-item
50 PRINT #4;A$             ;send each data-item
60 NEXT N
70 CLOSE #4
80 CLOSE #5
```

And, in the BBC microcomputer the following steps are suitable for receiving data over the RS423 link.

```
 10 *FX2,1              ;select RS423 input
 20 *FX3,6              ;select 'no output'
 30 *FX21,2             ;initialise RS423 buffer
 40 DIMA$(2)            ;there are three data-items
 50 FORN=0TO2
 60 INPUTR$             ;use R$ to collect the items
 70 LETA$(N)=R$         ;move items
 80 NEXT N
 90 *FX3,4              ;select screen output
100 *FX2,0              ;select keyboard input
...
110 PRINT A$(0),A$(1),A$(2)  ;the proof!
```

The above examples do show that it is indeed practical to use the **Microdrive** to store files for access by 'other' computers communicating with the **Spectrum** system via the RS232 link.

The final program:

If the user wishes to receive data byte-by-byte, rather than use **INPUT**, then the following BBC microcomputer program might be useful.

```
10 FX 2, 1 — select RS423 input *FX 2, 1
20 A% = 145
30 X% = 1
40 R = USR (&FFF4) — get a single byte
50 R = ( R AND &00FF0000) / 65536
60 IF R <> 0 THEN PRINT CHR$(R);
70 GOTO 10 — back for the next byte
```

Notes:

Line 50 — this isolates the ASCII value from the complex value returned by the USR function.

Line 60 — the value held in R can be manipulated in this or any other suitable manner.

This final program complements the BASIC program given in the section 'Extended use of the "T" system'; and can be used to handle 'output' sent over the **Spectrum**'s RS232 link.

Chapter 6

Using Machine Code

Author's note:
It is not intended that readers unfamiliar with Z80 machine code should read this chapter in detail. There are already many books available that teach machine code programming — including the author's **'Understanding Your Spectrum'** — and a good working knowledge of machine code programming is essential if the reader wishes to write his/her own routines.

It is also helpful to have to hand a machine code 'editor' program, or 'assembler'; and the 'SPDE' program from Campbell Systems remains the favourite of the author — it can be transferred to a **Microdrive** cartridge with ease and is very 'user friendly'. (Note that 'SPDE' is only an 'editor' and 'disassembler'; and is comparatively slow when compared to full 'assemblers'.)

Introduction:
This chapter is divided into two parts:

a. Using the Hook Codes
b. Adding new statements

as these two operations are totally distinct one from another.

a. Using the Hook Codes:
In the **Spectrum** system the Restart 0008h routine is used to handle errors. These errors are numbered and in the standard **Spectrum** have the range FFh to 1Ah. An error is handled by using a RST 0008h instruction followed by a DEFB (defined byte) set to the required value.

For example:

```
                ORG     7D00H   ;32000 DEC
7D00 CF  EXAM   RST     0008H   ;ERROR RESTART INSTRUCTION
7D01 0B         DEFB    0BH     ;GIVES 'NONSENSE IN BASIC'
                END
```

Which in BASIC would be:

POKE 32000,207:**POKE** 32001,11:**RANDOMISE USR** 32000

A DEFB of a value outside the normal range still gives an error situation but the report message is 'rubbish' as there are only appropriate messages for the values in range.

In a **Spectrum** fitted with a **ZX Interface 1** the 'shadow' ROM is paged-in by the instruction-fetch operation on location 0008h, and in the program of the 'shadow' ROM the value of the DEFB is considered further.

— DEFB's in the range 00h-1Ah are passed back.
— DEFB's in the range 1Bh-32h are the 'hook codes'.
— DEFB's in the range 33h-FEh give the 'shadow' error report 'Hook code error'.
— A DEFB that is FFh gives the 'shadow' error report 'Program finished' — that is a new feature.

The DEFB's in the range 1Bh-32h allow the user to call various subroutines in the 'shadow' ROM. That is, the use of — the instruction RST 0008h and the DEFB 'hook code' — is equivalent to — call 'shadow' ROM subroutine xxxx —.

In all cases when this operation is used, the 'shadow' ROM is paged-in, the subroutine executed, and the 'shadow' ROM paged-out. The user is never left with the 'shadow' ROM active.

The 'hook codes' 1Bh-32h will now be discussed in turn; but first note:

No registers are preserved — so take care to save register-values, such as counters, before using a hook code. Also: preserve H'L', the return address to BASIC, when using the more complex hook subroutines.

During all I/O transfers the maskable interrupt is 'off'; and certain hook subroutines 'turn off' this interrupt, whilst others require it 'off' before being called.

Hook code 32h is reserved by Sinclair Research Ltd.

Hook code 31h 'inserts' the new system variables and should be used whenever this is required (see below).

Hook code 1Bh — Console input:
This subroutine waits for a key to be pressed on the keyboard of the **Spectrum**. Then, when a key is pressed, the character code is found and

returned in the A register. The maskable interrupt must be 'on'.
Keystrokes that do not give character codes are ignored.

It can be used as follows:

```
              ORG    7D00H    ;32000 DEC
7D00 3E02  CON#IN LD  A,02H   ;PRINT TO UPPER PART OF T.V
7D02 CD0116       CALL 1601H  ;CALL SELECT (CHAN#OPEN)
7D05 06FF         LD  B,0FFH  ;SET A COUNTER
7D07 C5    EACH  PUSH BC      ;SAVE COUNTER
7D08 CF           RST  0008H  ;CALL 'CONSOLE INPUT' TO
7D09 1B           DEFB 1BH    ;FETCH EACH CHARACTER CODE
7D0A C1           POP  BC     ;RESTORE COUNTER
7D0B D7           RST  0010H  ;PRINT CHARACTER
7D0C 10F9         DJNZ EACH   ;LOOP BACK
7D0E C9           RET         ;FINISHED
                  END
```

In the above example the keyboard is read '255' times and the character echoed to the screen.

HOOK CODE 1Ch — CONSOLE OUTPUT

This subroutine performs the same operations as — LD A,02h, CALL SELECT & RST 0010h, i.e. the character presently held in the A register is printed using stream '2' — normally the upper part of the TV screen. Note that scrolling is suppressed. The previous example can be rewritten as:

```
              ORG    7D00H    ;32000 DEC
7D00 06FF  CON#OUT LD B,0FFH  ;SET A COUNTER
7D02 C5    EACH  PUSH BC      ;SAVE COUNTER
7D03 CF           RST  0008H  ;CALL 'CONSOLE INPUT' TO
7D04 1B           DEFB 1BH    ;FETCH EACH CHARACTER CODE
7D05 CF           RST  0008H  ;CALL 'CONSOLE OUTPUT' TO
7D06 1C           DEFB 1CH    ;PRINT EACH CHARACTER
7D07 C1           POP  BC     ;RESTORE COUNTER
7D08 10F8         DJNZ EACH   ;LOOP BACK
7D0A C9           RET         ;FINISHED
                  END
```

HOOK CODE 1Dh — RS232 INPUT:

This subroutine accepts bytes of data via the RS232 link. The 'data transfer rate' is controlled by the value of BAUD; and the border colour by the value in IOBORD.
It is best to clear SER_FL before collecting the first byte just in case a 'late' character is still held.

The example shows characters being received using this hook code.

Remember that SER_FL does not exist before 'shadow' system variable insertion — use hook code 31h if required (see below)

```
                    ORG    7D00H         ;32000 DEC
7D00 AF     RS#IN   XOR    A             ;CLEAR A REGISTER
7D01 32C75C         LD     (SER#FL),A    ;CLEAR SER#FL
7D04 06FF           LD     B,0FFH        ;SET A COUNTER
7D06 C5     EACH    PUSH   BC            ;SAVE COUNTER
7D07 CF             RST    0008H         ;CALL 'RS232 INPUT' TO FETCH
7D08 1D             DEFB   1DH           ; THE CHARACTERS
7D09 CF             RST    0008H         ;USE 'CONSOLE OUTPUT' TO
7D0A 1C             DEFB   1CH           ;PRINT THE CHARACTERS
7D0B C1             POP    BC            ;RESTORE COUNTER
7D0C 10F8           DJNZ   EACH          ;LOOP BACK
7D0E C9             RET                  ;FINISHED
                    END
```

HOOK CODE 1Eh — RS232 OUTPUT:

This is the corresponding output subroutine. Again, BAUD determines the 'data transfer rate' and IOBORD the border colour. As usual no data byte will be sent unless DTR is holding a high signal.

The following example complements the example for RS232 input.

```
                    ORG    7D00H         ;32000 DEC
7D00 06FF   RS#OUT  LD     B,0FFH        ;SET A COUNTER
7D02 C5     EACH    PUSH   BC            ;SAVE COUNTER
7D03 3E41           LD     A,41H         ;CHARACTER 'A'
7D05 CF             RST    0008H         ;USE 'RS232 OUTPUT' TO SEND
7D06 1E             DEFB   1EH           ;'255' A'S
7D07 C1             POP    BC            ;RESTORE COUNTER
7D08 10F8           DJNZ   EACH          ;LOOP BACK
7D0A C9             RET                  ;FINISHED
                    END
```

The example sends a set of '255' bytes each of which is of value 41h.

HOOK CODE 1Fh — ZX PRINTER OUTPUT:
This subroutine is identical to 'console output' except for the use of stream '3' instead of stream '2'. The output normally therefore goes to the ZX printer.

HOOK CODE 20h — KEYBOARD TEST:
This subroutine uses the following instructions to test for a key depression:

```
AF              XOR   A              ;CLEAR THE A REGISTER
DBFE            IN    A,(0FEH)       ;READ 8 LINES OF KEYBOARD
E61F            AND   1FH            ;KEEP LOWER 5 DATA BITS
D61F            SUB   1FH            ;NO-KEY=0
                                     ;ANY-KEY='MINUS'
C6FF            ADD   A,0FFH         ;NO-KEY='CARRY RESET'
                                     ;ANY-KEY='CARRY SET'
                END
```

The use of — RST 0008h & DEFB 20h — instead of the above five instructions does not really offer any advantage.

HOOK CODE 21H — SELECT DRIVE
This is the first of thirteen hook codes that refer to the **Microdrive**.

The 'Select drive' subroutine starts the motor in a specified **Microdrive** unit; with the **Microdrive** being numbered 1 — 8. Selecting drive '0' turns off all **Microdrive** unit motors. The subroutine returns with the maskable interrupt turned 'off' if a drive motor is started.

This subroutine will lead to the generation of the report '**Microdrive** not present' if the operation cannot be performed correctly.

For example; **Microdrive** drive motor '1' can be started by:

```
                        ORG   7D00H          ;32000 DEC
7D00 3E01       SEL#DR  LD    A,01H          ;CONTROL MICRODRIVE '1'
7D02 CF                 RST   0008H          ;CALL 'SELECT DRIVE'
7D03 21                 DEFB  21H
7D04 FB                 EI                   ;ENABLE INTERRUPTS
7D05 C9                 RET                  ;FINISHED
                        END
```

(The drive motor can be stopped from BASIC by creating any error report; e.g. **CAT** & **ENTER**.)

HOOK CODE 22h — OPEN FILE:
This hook code allows the machine code programmer to create an 'ad hoc' **Microdrive** channel; with the base address of the channel being returned in the IX register pair.
The hook code is used as follows:
— ensure the 'shadow' system variables exist (if needed using hook code 31H — see below)
— save the values of H'L'
— enter the drive number into D_STR1
— write a filename into suitable location(s)
— enter the descriptor of the filename into N_STR1; in the order i. low length, ii. high length, iii. low starting address, and iv. high starting address
— call 'Open file'
... restore H'L' before returning to BASIC

The hook code can only be used to create a channel for a 'data file'; and performs actions similar to the **OPEN** command.
— **IF** the filename is a new and **THEN** the file is open for 'writing',
— **ELSE** the file is for 'reading' and the first record is found and loaded

And, once created the file can be manipulated as follows:
— Make **Microdrive** channel the current channel, i.e. use PUSH IX, POP HL, LD (CURCHL), HL.

then either:
— write to a file using RST 0010h; with the characters in the A register
— read from the file by using CALL 15E6 (INCH or INPUT-AD).

Note that 'writing' the 513th, 1025th, . . . character will lead to a further record being created; and similarly during 'reading' further records are fetched as required.

An example of the use of 'Open file' is given in the discussion of 'Close file' which follows.

HOOK CODE 23h — CLOSE FILE:
The actions of this subroutine are very similar to the effect of using **CLOSE**; associated with a **Microdrive** 'data file'. If the file, whose base address is in the IX register pair, is open for 'writing' then any data as yet 'unsent' goes to form an 'end of file' record; and the channel is reclaimed. But when the file is for 'reading', any data in its data area is lost; and the channel is reclaimed.

The following example shows the creation of a channel for a file 'a' on **Microdrive** '1'. The file is then 'written-to' or 'read-from' before being 'closed'.

```
              ORG     7D00H           ;32000 DEC
       NAME   EQU     7CFFH           ;WILL HOLD 'A'
CF     COMMON RST     0008H           ;CREATE SYSTEM VARIABLES
31            DEFB    31H             ; IN CASE NONEXISTENT
D9            EXX
E5            PUSH    HL              ;SAVE VALUES OF HL'
D9            EXX
3E01          LD      A,01H           ;SELECT DRIVE '1'
32D65C        LD      (D#STR1),A
3E61          LD      A,61H           ;FILENAME TO BE 'A'
32FF7C        LD      (NAME),A
210100        LD      HL,0001H        ;'A' IS SINGLE CHARACTER
22DA5C        LD      (N#STR1),HL
21FF7C        LD      HL,NAME         ;ADDRESS START IS NAME
22DC5C        LD      (N#STR1+02H),HL
       ;
CF     FILE   RST     0008H           ;CALL 'OPEN FILE'
22            DEFB    22H
DDE5          PUSH    IX              ;MAKE MICRODRIVE CHANNEL
E1            POP     HL              ;THE CURRENT CHANNEL
22515C        LD      (CURCHL),HL
       ;A FILE OF '3000' BYTES IS EITHER CREATED OR READ
01B80B        LD      BC,0BB8H        ;3000 DEC
C5     EACH   PUSH    BC              ;SAVE COUNTER
       ;WHEN 'WRITING' - ENTER THE FOLLOWING BYTES
3E41          LD      A,41H           ;FILE WILL HOLD
D7            RST     0010H           ;3000 A'S
       ;WHEN 'READING' - ENTER THE FOLLOWING BYTES
CDE615        CALL    INCH            ;FETCH A CHARACTER CODE
CF            RST     0008H           ;USE 'CONSOLE OUTPUT'
1C            DEFB    1CH
DDE5          PUSH    IX              ;MAKE MICRODRIVE CHANNEL
E1            POP     HL              ;THE CURRENT CHANNEL AGAIN
22515C        LD      (CURCHL),HL
       ;CONTINUE WITH
C1            POP     BC              ;FETCH COUNTER
0B            DEC     BC              ;DECREASE COUNTER
78            LD      A,B             ;HAS COUNTER REACHED ZERO?
```

Enter only one of following blocks of code depending on whether you are 'writing' or 'reading'.

```
B1              OR    C
20 --           JR    NZ,EACH       ;BACK IF NOT ZERO YET
CF              RST   0008H         ;CALL 'CLOSE FILE'        Value of relative
23              DEFB  23H                                     jump is different
3E02            LD    A,02H         ;RESELECT T.V SCREEN      for 'writing' and
CD0116          CALL  SELECT                                  'reading'.
D9              EXX                 ;FETCH THE SAVED VALUES
E1              POP   HL            ;OF HL'
D9              EXX
C9              RET                 ;FINISHED
                END
```

The reader should first use the above example to create a new file 'a' on drive '1'; and then read the data back. The jump is '20 F6' when 'writing' and '20 EE' when 'reading'.

HOOK CODE 24h — DELETE FILE:

This subroutine can be used to 'erase' a named file from a **Microdrive** cartridge. The parameters of the file have to be prepared in D_STR1 & N_STR1. Both 'program files' and 'data files' can be 'erased' by this hook subroutine. For example the file 'a' on drive '1' can be 'erased' as follows: (But keep a copy for later, by using for example **MOVE** "m",1;"a" **TO** "m";1;"b")

```
                ORG   7D00H         ;32000 DEC
          NAME  EQU   7CFFH         ;WILL HOLD 'A'
          ;ENTER 13 INSTRUCTION LINES OF COMMON - SEE 'CLOSE FILE'
7D1B CF   DELETE RST  0008H         ;CALL 'DELETE FILE'
7D1C 24         DEFB  24H
7D1D D9         EXX
7D1E E1         POP   HL            ;RESTORE HL'
7D1F D9         EXX
7D20 C9         RET                 ;FINISHED
                END
```

HOOK CODE 25h — READ SEQUENTIAL:

This hook code allows the user to fetch the 'next record' of a named 'data file' into the data work space of its **Microdrive** channel.

On entry to the subroutine the IX register pair must hold the base address of the **Microdrive** channel and the channel variable CHREC the number of the 'present record'. CHREC will always be incremented.

The following example shows the six records of the test file "a" being fetched in order:

```
                    ORG     7D00H           ;32000 DEC
7CFF        NAME.   EQU     7CFFH           ;WILL HOLD 'A'
                    ;ENTER 13 INSTRUCTION LINES OF COMMON - SEE 'CLOSE FILE'
7D1B CF     READSQ  RST     0008H           ;CALL 'OPEN FILE'
7D1C 22             DEFB    22H
7D1D CD407D EACH    CALL    REC#NO          ;PRINT THE RECORD-NUMBER
7D20 CF             RST     0008H           ;CALL 'READ SEQUENTIAL'
7D21 25             DEFB    25H
7D22 18F9           JR      EACH            ;FOR EACH RECORD
                ;
                    ORG     7D40H           ;32064 DEC
                    ;THE RECORD-NUMBER PRINTING SUBROUTINE
7D40 DD7E44 REC#NO  LD      A,(IX+44H)      ;COLLECT THE PRESENT RECNUM
7D43 C630           ADD     A,30H           ;FORM ASCII
7D45 CF             RST     0008H           ;CALL 'CONSOLE OUTPUT'
7D46 1C             DEFB    1CH
7D47 DDE5           PUSH    IX              ;MAKE MICRODRIVE CHANNEL
7D49 E1             POP     HL              ; CURRENT AGAIN
7D4A 22515C         LD      (CURCHL),HL
7D4D C9             RET                     ;FINISHED
                    END
```

The above example only produced the result "012345" but this does show that the records have indeed been fetched — although not read. Note how the example finishes at 'end of file'.

HOOK CODE 26h — WRITE RECORD:
This hook code allows the user to create a record. As usual the IX register pair has to hold the base address of the **Microdrive** channel that contains the data for the record. The record will be created in the next free sector on the **Microdrive** tape.

For example:

```
                    ORG     7D00H           ;32000 DEC
            NAME    EQU     7CFFH           ;WILL HOLD 'A' - OR OTHER
            ;ENTER THE LINES OF THE 'CLOSE FILE' EXAMPLE - FOR
            ;'WRITING' BUT CHANGE  LD BC,0BBBH  TO  LD BC,0200H
            ;AND    CF 23  'CLOSE FILE'  TO  CF 26  'WRITE FILE'
            ;CHANGE THE NAME OF THE FILE IF USING A CARTRIDGE THAT
            ;ALREADY HOLDS A FILE 'A'
                    END
```

It is sensible to use 'close file' when writing the 'end of file' record.

HOOK CODE 27h — READ RANDOM:
This subroutine is similar to 'read sequential' but the record fetched is the CHREC-record.

HOOK CODE 28h —READ SECTOR:
This subroutine fetches the record from the sector specified by CHREC. The carry flag will be returned reset if the checksum of the data is correct; and set otherwise. The user has to select the **Microdrive** unit before using this hook code (or the next two).

HOOK CODE 29h — READ NEXT:
This subroutine fetches the record from the 'next' sector that passes the READ head of the **Microdrive** unit. The sector's number will be available in HDNUMB. Again the carry flag is returned reset only if the checksum on the data proves correct. Note that there is insufficient time between sectors to 'fetch' and 'move' a whole record before the following header block is reached; hence records for a named file are never in contiguous sectors.

HOOK CODE 2Ah — WRITE SECTOR:
This subroutine performs the opposite action to 'read sector'. The data currently held in the data buffer is copied to the sector whose number is specified by CHREC.

HOOK CODE 2Bh — CREATE BUFFER:
This subroutine should create a **Microdrive** channel (and a map area) for the file specified by D_STR1 & N_STR1. However due to a programming error this hook code has the same effect as 'open file'. (This may be corrected in later 'shadow' ROMs).

The following example shows, however, how a **Microdrive** channel and map area can be created.

```
7C80                    ORG     7C80H           ;31872 DEC
                ;CHANNEL BYTES
7C80 08                 DEFB    08H
7C81 00                 DEFB    00H
7C82 08                 DEFB    08H
7C83 00                 DEFB    00H
7C84 CD                 DEFB    0CDH            ;CD IS 'M' + 80H
7C85 D8                 DEFB    0D8H            ;('AD HOC' BUFFER)
7C86 11                 DEFB    11H
7C87 22                 DEFB    22H
```

```
7C88 11            DEFB   11H
7C89 53            DEFB   53H
7C8A 02            DEFB   02H
7C8B 00            DEFB   00H
7C8C 00            DEFB   00H
7C8D 00            DEFB   00H
7C8E 61            DEFB   61H           ;FILENAME 'A'
7C8F 20            DEFB   20H
7C90 20            DEFB   20H
7C91 20            DEFB   20H
7C92 20            DEFB   20H
7C93 20            DEFB   20H
7C94 20            DEFB   20H
7C95 20            DEFB   20H
7C96 20            DEFB   20H
7C97 20            DEFB   20H
7C98 FF            DEFB   0FFH          ;FF IS 'OPEN FOR WRITE'
7C99 01            DEFB   01H           ;01 IS FOR MICRODRIVE '1'
7C9A 00            DEFB   00H
7C9B 00            DEFB   00H
7C9C 00            DEFB   00H
7C9D 00            DEFB   00H
7C9E 00            DEFB   00H
7C9F 00            DEFB   00H
7CA0 00            DEFB   00H
7CA1 00            DEFB   00H
7CA2 00            DEFB   00H
7CA3 00            DEFB   00H
7CA4 00            DEFB   00H
7CA5 00            DEFB   00H
7CA6 FF            DEFB   0FFH
7CA7 FF            DEFB   0FFH          ;FF FF IS END OF HEADER
7CA8 00            DEFB   00H           ;PREAMBLE
7CA9 00            DEFB   00H
7CAA 00            DEFB   00H
7CAB 00            DEFB   00H
7CAC 00            DEFB   00H
7CAD 00            DEFB   00H

                   ;CHMAP ARE THE TWO BYTES UNDERLINED AND WILL HAVE TO BE
                   ;SET SEPARATELY
```

```
7CAE  00                DEFB    00H
7CAF  00                DEFB    00H
7CB0  00                DEFB    00H
7CB1  00                DEFB    00H
7CB2  00                DEFB    00H
7CB3  00                DEFB    00H
7CB4  00                DEFB    00H
7CB5  00                DEFB    00H
7CB6  00                DEFB    00H
7CB7  00                DEFB    00H
7CB8  00                DEFB    00H
7CB9  00                DEFB    00H
7CBA  00                DEFB    00H
7CBB  00                DEFB    00H
7CBC  00                DEFB    00H
7CBD  00                DEFB    00H
7CBE  00                DEFB    00H
7CBF  00                DEFB    00H
7CC0  00                DEFB    00H
7CC1  FF                DEFB    0FFH
7CC2  FF                DEFB    0FFH          ;FF FF IS END OF DATA
                                              ;BLOCK PREAMBLE
                        ORG     7D00H         ;32000 DEC
7D00  2A4F5C    START   LD      HL,(CHANS)    ;FIRST CREATE A MAP AREA
7D03  E5                PUSH    HL            ;SAVE BASE ADDRESS
7D04  2B                DEC     HL
7D05  012000            LD      BC,0020H      ;'32' LOCATIONS
7D08  CD5516            CALL    MAKEROOM      ;CREATE THE MAP AREA
7D0B  E1                POP     HL
7D0C  E5                PUSH    HL            ;COPY BASE ADDRESS
7D0D  AF                XOR     A             ;MAP BITS TO BE ALL RESET
7D0E  0620              LD      B,20H
7D10  77        EACH#ONE LD     (HL),A
7D11  23                INC     HL
7D12  10FC              DJNZ    EACH#ONE
                ;THE BASE ADDRESS OF THE MAP AREA IS ON THE MACHINE
                ;STACK. THE CHANNEL CAN NOW BE CREATED.
7D14  2A535C            LD      HL,(PROG)     ;BEFORE PROG.
7D17  2B                DEC     HL
7D18  E5                PUSH    HL
7D19  E5                PUSH    HL            ;TAKE TWO COPIES
```

```
7D1A DDE1                POP      IX              ;ONE FOR IX
7D1C 015302              LD       BC,0253H        ;LENGTH OF CHANNEL
7D1F CD5516              CALL     MAKEROOM        ;CREATE THE CHANNEL AREA
7D22 21807C              LD       HL,7C80H        ;NOW COPY OVER THE
7D25 D1                  POP      DE              ;CHANNEL BYTES GIVEN ABOVE
7D26 014300              LD       BC,0043H        ;'67' OF THEM
7D29 EDB0                LDIR
                         ;NOW FILL IN CHMAP
7D2B E1                  POP      HL              ;FETCH THE ADDRESS
7D2C DD751A              LD       (IX+CHMAP),L
7D2F DD741B              LD       (IX+CHMAP+01H),H
7D32 C9                  RET                      ;FINISHED
                         END
```

HOOK CODE 2Ch - DELETE BUFFER:
This subroutine is most straightforward. The channel (and its map) whose base address is held in the IX register pair is reclaimed. All the 'higher' dynamic areas are thereby moved down by '627' bytes.

HOOK CODE 2Dh — OPEN NETWORK CHANNEL:
This is the first of four hook codes for accessing subroutines that deal with the local area network. The first subroutine creates a 'B' network channel. The 'destination' station number is to be in D_STR1; and the SELF station number in NTSTAT.

As usual the base address of the new channel is returned in the IX register pair. Bytes of data can be sent or received using this channel — with RST 0010h or CALL 15E6 — once the channel has been made 'current'. (See example below.)

HOOK CODE 2Eh — CLOSE NETWORK CHANNEL:
This subroutine can be used to close a network channel whose base address is in the IX register pair. If the channel has been used for 'sending' then any 'unsent' data will be marked 'end of file' and 'sent'; but in a 'receiving' channel any unused data is discarded.

The following example shows data being 'sent' over the network using machine code (from station '1', to station '2').

```
                         ORG      7D00H           ;32000 DEC
7D00 21D65C  STRT#OUT    LD       HL,D#STR1
7D03 3602                LD       (HL),02H        ;DESTINATION '2'
7D05 CF                  RST      0008H           ;'OPEN NETWORK CHANNEL'
7D06 2D                  DEFB     2DH
7D07 DDE5                PUSH     IX              ;MAKE THE NEW CHANNEL
7D09 E1                  POP      HL              ;'CURRENT'
```

```
7D0A 22515C           LD      (CURCHL),HL
                      ;SEND SOME BYTES OF DATA - FOR EXAMPLE:
7D0D 013412           LD      BC,1234H
7D10 C5       EACH#OUT PUSH   BC
7D11 79               LD      A,C
7D12 D7               RST     PRINTA1
7D13 C1               POP     BC
7D14 0B               DEC     BC
7D15 79               LD      A,C
7D16 B0               OR      B
7D17 20F7             JR      NZ,EACH#OUT
                      ;NOW SIGNAL 'END OF FILE'
7D19 CF               RST     0008H          ;'CLOSE NETWORK CHANNEL'
7D1A 2E               DEFB    2EH
7D1B C9               RET                    ;FINISHED
                      END
```

And, the data can be received as follows (by station '1', from station '2'):

```
                      ORG     7D00H          ;32000 DEC
7D00 21065C   STARTIN LD      HL,D#STR1      ;IRIS IS AGAIN '2'
7D03 3602             LD      (HL),02H
7D05 CF               RST     0008H          ;'OPEN NETWORK CHANNEL'
7D06 2D               DEFB    2DH
                      ;EACH BYTE IS RECIEVED IN TURN
7D07 DDE5     EACH#IN PUSH    IX             ;MAKE CHANNEL 'CURRENT'
7D09 E1               POP     HL
7D0A 22515C           LD      (CURCHL),HL
7D0D DDE5             PUSH    IX             ;IX IS CORRUPTED BY INCH
                                             ;WHEN USING THE NETWORK
7D0F CDE615   TRY     CALL    INCH           ;TRY FETCHING A BYTE
7D12 30FB             JR      NC,TRY         ;BACK IF STATION '2' IS
                                             ;NOT LOOKING FOR '1'
7D14 FE20             CP      ' '            ;'CONSOLE OUT' DOES NOT
7D16 38F7             JR      C,TRY          ;LIKE CONTROL CODES
7D18 DDE1             POP     IX             ;IX RETRIEVED AFTER INCH
7D1A CF               RST     0008H          ;'CONSOLE OUTPUT'
7D1B 1C               DEFB    1CH
7D1C 18E9             JR      EACH#IN        ;NEVER ENDING!
                      END
```

The network channel can be reclaimed by using 'close network channel' in a finite situation.

Hook code 2Fh — Get packet:
This subroutine allows the user to fetch a particular SCOUT, HEADER & 'data block'. The net channel variables NCIRIS, NCSELF & NCNUMB have to have the necessary values. The subroutine will return carry-set if 'time-out' occurs or the checksums fail to be correct. As usual there is no 'time-out' when awaiting a broadcast.

Hook code 30h — Send packet:
This subroutine allows the user to send a SCOUT, HEADER and 'data block'. On entry the A register is to hold zero for an ordinary block of data; and '1' for an 'end of file' block. Both this hook and the previous one will cause NCNUMB to be advanced if they are successful.

Hook code 31h — Create system variables:
This is a 'dummy' hook code and can be used to ensure that the 'shadow' system variables are 'inserted'. The following BASIC program shows this hook code in use.

```
NEW & ENTER
 10 PRINT "Before"
 20 FOR A= 23734 TO 23791
 30 PRINT PEEK A;" ";
 40 NEXT A
 50 POKE 32000,207          — RST 0008h
 60 POKE 32001,49           — 'create system variables'
 70 POKE 32002,201          — RET
 80 RANDOMIZE USR 32000
 90 PRINT '
100 PRINT "after"
110 FOR A=23734 TO 23791
120 PRINT PEEK A;" ";
130 NEXT A
RUN & ENTER
```

Remember the system variables are only inserted once and cannot, thereafter, be removed. If needed **SAVE** the above program on cassette (not Microdrive) and enter **NEW** before re-**LOAD**ing.

b. Adding New Statements

It is possible by using machine code to add new statements to the **Spectrum's** BASIC — when using a **Spectrum** fitted with a **ZX Interface 1**. This is feasible as the user can change the address in the 'shadow' system variable VECTOR and thereby break into the BASIC interpreter. The 'rules' governing the addition of new statements are complicated but once understood some useful statements can be produced.

The BASIC interpreter in the 'main' ROM:
In the first instance it will be useful to discuss how BASIC statements are handled by the machine code program resident in the 'main' ROM of the **Spectrum**.

There are three stages involved:

a. The user enters a 'tentative' BASIC line into the 'edit buffer'. (This line is displayed with tokens expanded in the lower part of the TV display.) The BASIC line is made up of a set of BASIC statements — for simplicity it is best to consider single-statement lines from now on in the discussion.

b. The pressing of the **ENTER** key signals that the user wishes to have the 'tentative' line considered for the correctness of its syntax. In testing the syntax of a statement the BASIC interpreter first identifies the 'command' of the statement (e.g. **PRINT** from a statement such as 10 **PRINT** 4+2). Next the 'command routine' for that command is executed — but only as far as is required for checking syntax.

IF the syntax of the statement is correct **THEN** the statement is accepted; and goes to its correct place in the program area (assuming a single-statement line starting with a line number). The 'editor' is called for the next line to be entered.

ELSE a jump is made to the 'error handling routine' — using a RST 0008h instruction followed by a DEFB that shows the error type. This will lead to the 'editor' being called again and the 'tentative' line displayed with the 'syntax error marker'.

c. The third stage involves the 'execution' of a statement (the so-called 'run-time' operation).
In run-time the 'command' of a BASIC statement has again to be identified. Next, the 'command routine' is found and executed.

IF the statement is executed without error **THEN** the next statement is considered.

ELSE the 'error handling routine' will be called but this time a 'run-time' error report will be displayed in the lower part of the TV screen.

From the above discussion it follows that for a statement to be 'acceptable' and 'executable' there must be the necessary 'syntax' and 'run-time' parts of a 'command routine' for the command of the statement.

The BASIC interpreter in the 'shadow' ROM:
The machine code program in the 'shadow' ROM forms an extension to the 'main' ROM program; and is called into use every time the 'error handling routine' is entered.

The 'shadow' program allows for a 'second thought' about the 'error' that occurred in the 'main' program; and it is thereby possible to provide the 'syntax & run-time' command routines that handle the **Microdrive**, Local area network and RS232 link.

In the 'shadow' ROM program there are routines to handle statements that start with:
CAT, FORMAT, MOVE, ERASE, OPEN, SAVE, LOAD, VERIFY, MERGE, CLS, & **CLEAR**
(**CLOSE** is handled separately as it has its own 'paging' address)

A simplified view of the path through the 'shadow' ROM program can be considered to be:
- In the case of an error, identify the command of the statement.
- **IF** the command is not in the above list **THEN** return to the 'main' ROM program via the address held in VECTOR.
- **ELSE** jump to the appropriate command routine — leaving it via ST_END in syntax time, END1 in run-time, Restart ROMERR if giving a 'main' error report and Restart SH_ERR if giving a 'shadow' error report — in all cases a return is made to the 'main' ROM program.

THE SYNTAX OF NEW STATEMENTS:
When the user wishes to add a new statement to the BASIC of the **Spectrum** it is necessary to define a statement which 'fails' the syntax of both the 'main' and the 'shadow' ROM programs. Note that such a statement cannot start with any of the eleven commands for which there are command routines in the 'shadow' ROM program (see above).

There are a great many statements that could be defined, although the author would suggest that the reader tries a variety of simple statements before embarking on any complex statements.

The following list contains examples of suitable statements:

Using **LINE** — not normally a command but can be made to be one.
e.g. 10 **LINE** — may draw a particular line.

Using **DRAW** — with a new set of parameters.
e.g. 10 **DRAW** n — may underline 'n' characters.

Using **CIRCLE** — with a new set of parameters.
e.g. 10 **CIRCLE** n — may draw a circle of diameter 'n'.

Using **BORDER** — with a new set of parameters.
e.g. 10 **BORDER** *b,i,p — the separator '*' prevents any 'main' ROM actions. The statement might change the **BORDER**, **INK** & **PAPER** colours in a certain manner.

The above are only suggestions. Remember it is possible to use anything that 'fails' the existing syntax (& run-time) checking procedure.

USING THE 'SHADOW' SYSTEM VARIABLE — VECTOR:

The first point to be made about this system variable is that it normally holds (after 'insertion') the value 01F0h (496 dec.). This is the 'shadow' address known as ERR_6.
 — This can be shown by entering:
CAT & **ENTER** (or anything else that ensures 'insertion')
PRINT PEEK 23735+256***PEEK** 23736

The actual lines from the 'shadow' ROM program that use VECTOR are:

```
ERR_V   LD HL, (VECTOR)    ;fetch the vectored address
        JP (HL)            ;this is normally ERR_6
ERR_6   ......             ;allow existing error through
```

The 'shadow' system variable VECTOR normally holds the address ERR_6 (01F0h) and this acts as a vectored address.

The first stage to adding new statements is the changing of the contents of VECTOR so as to allow for further tests to be made on the error-statement.

The following BASIC example shows the address held in VECTOR changed; so that the routine EXTEND is included.

CAT & **ENTER** — ensure 'insertion'
10 **POKE** 23735,0 — VECTOR is to hold **7D00h**
20 **POKE** 23736,125 — (32000 dec.)
30 **POKE** 32000,195 — These three numbers are
40 **POKE** 32001,240 — the EXTEND routine
50 **POKE** 32002,1 — only JP ERR_6
RUN & **ENTER** ;and the **Spectrum** should not crash!

USING THE POINTER CH ADD:
CH_ADD (character address) is the 'main' system variable held in locations 5C5Dh & 5C5Eh (23645/6 dec.); and it is used to address the characters of a statement. On entry to the routine EXTEND the system variable CH_ADD points to the command of the error-statement.

The two 'main' ROM routines — Restart 0018h, GET_CHAR and Restart 0020h, NEXT_CHAR — return to the user, in the A register, the current character addressed by CH_ADD and the next character, respectively. Both routines ignore space characters and control codes.

GET_CHAR and NEXT_CHAR are very useful routines as they provide a suitable manner of manipulating CH_ADD.

THE CALBAS SUBROUTINE:
The CALBAS subroutine is located at 'shadow' address 0010h (16 dec.) and can be called using the instructions RST 0010h. This subroutine allows the user to call a 'main' ROM subroutine whilst the 'shadow' ROM is 'paged-in'.

The instruction RST 0010h has to be followed by the address of the 'main' subroutine required.

E.g. To call GET CHAR whilst the 'shadow' ROM is in use:

```
D7              RST     CALBAS
1800            DEFW    GET#CHAR
                END
```

Note that all registers are returned as normal from the 'main' subroutine.

SYNTAX & RUN-TIME MODULES:
The command routine that is to be added to handle a 'new statement' has to have two parts:
a. The syntax module
The steps involved in checking the syntax of a statement involves the identification of:
- the command
- any necessary separators
- numeric expressions
- string expressions
- variables

and finally:
- the end of the statement
which will be a ':' or a 'carriage return'

The subroutines that can be used to help in these steps will be discussed in the examples that follow.

b. The run-time module
In this module the actual 'work' of the statement is performed and this will depend on the statement being implemented.

Actual 'new statements':
A set of 'new statements' will now be discussed in detail:

LINE
A statement that 'frames' the current display mimicing the line:
PLOT 0,0: **DRAW** 255,0; **DRAW** 0,175: **DRAW** -255,0: **DRAW** 0,-175

The syntax module:
In the first instance the command has to be handled by:
- Fetch the command code — using GET_CHAR
- Compare the code to **LINE** (CAh/202 dec.)
  IF the code fails to match **THEN** jump to ERR_6
  ELSE proceed to the syntax module proper.
- Advance CH_ADD past the command — using NEXT_CHAR
- Call the ST_END routine so as to confirm the end of the statement; and 'accept' the statement in syntax time.

In assembly language this is:

```
                        ORG     7D00H           ;32000 DEC
7D00  D7        EXTEND  RST     CALBAS
7D01  1800              DEFW    GET#CHAR        ;FETCH THE COMMAND CODE
7D03  FECA              CP      LINE            ;IS IT LINE?
7D05  CA207D            JP      Z,LINE#SYN      ;JUMP IF SO
7D08  C3F001            JP      ERR#6           ;LET ERROR THROUGH
                ;
7D20                    ORG     7D20H           ;LINE STATEMENT
                                                ;SYNTAX MODULE

7D20  D7        LINE#SYN RST    CALBAS
7D21  2000              DEFW    NXT#CHAR        ;ADVANCE CH#ADD
7D23  CDB705            CALL    ST#END          ;CONFIRM END OF STATEMENT &
                                                ;EXIT IN SYNTAX TIME
                ;TEMPORARY RUN-TIME MODULE
7D26  C3C105    LINE#RUN JP     END1            ;EXIT - NO WORK DONE
                        END
```

The reader is advised to enter the above twenty bytes of code, change the value in VECTOR and try the statement —

LINE — before proceeding to consider the run-time module that follows.

The run-time module:
The LINE#RUN routine to produce a 'frame' that goes around the edge of the T.V. display is:

```
                ORG     7D26H               ;32038 DEC
7D26 210000     LINE#RUN LD  HL,0000H       ;MAKE LAST PLOTTED POSITION
7D29 227D5C     LD      (COORDS),HL         ;0,0
7D2C 01FF00     LD      BC,00FFH
7D2F 110101     LD      DE,0101H
7D32 D7         RST     CALBAS
7D33 BA24       DEFW    DRAW#3              ;DRAW 255,0
7D35 0100AF     LD      BC,0AF00H
7D38 110101     LD      DE,0101H
7D3B D7         RST     CALBAS
7D3C BA24       DEFW    DRAW#3              ;DRAW 0,175
7D3E 01FF00     LD      BC,00FFH
7D41 11FFFF     LD      DE,0FFFFH
7D44 D7         RST     CALBAS
7D45 BA24       DEFW    DRAW#3              ;DRAW -255,0
7D47 0100AF     LD      BC,0AF00H
7D4A 11FFFF     LD      DE,0FFFFH
7D4D D7         RST     CALBAS
7D4E BA24       DEFW    24BAH               ;DRAW 0,-175
7D50 C3C105     JP      END1                ;EXIT IN RUN-TIME
                END
```

In the above routine there are four calls to the DRAW 3 subroutine that draws a line from the 'current position' to a position B_C away. The DE register pair holds SGN y and SGN x, respectively.

DRAW n
The second new statement to be discussed allows the user to underline a specified number of characters. The statement mimics the line:
    PRINT OVER 1; "____ . . . ____";
and 'n' specifies the number of 'underline' characters used. The range of 'n' will be from 1 to 255.

The syntax module:

The steps are:
- Fetch the command code — using GET_CHAR
- Compare the code **DRAW** (FCh/252 dec.)
- Proceed to the syntax module proper if the codes match.
- Advance CH_ADD past the command — using NEXT_CHAR
- Look for a 'numeric expression' — using EXPT_1NUM
  (expect an expression which must prove to be numeric)
- Call the ST_END routine so as to confirm the ending of the statement; and 'accept' the statement in syntax time.

In assembly language this is:

```
                    ORG    7D00H              ;32000 DEC
7D00 D7     EXTEND  RST    CALBAS
7D01 1800           DEFW   GET#CHAR           ;GET COMMAND CODE
            ;FORM A SEQUENTIAL 'COMMAND SEARCH'
7D03 FECA           CP     LINE
7D05 CA207D         JP     Z,LINE#SYN         ;FOR LINE
            ;
7D08 FEFC           CP     DRAW
7D0A CA607D         JP     Z,DRAW#SYN         ;FOR DRAW N
            ;
7D0D C3F001         JP     ERR#6              ;END OF 'SEARCH'
            ;DRAW N - SYNTAX MODULE PROPER
7D60                ORG    7D60H              ;32096 DEC
7D60 D7     DRAW#SYN RST   CALBAS
7D61 2000           DEFW   NXT#CHAR           ;ADVANCE CH#ADD
7D63 D7             RST    CALBAS
7D64 821C           DEFW   EXPT#1NM           ;FIND A NUMERIC
                                              ;EXPRESSION
7D66 CDB705         CALL   ST#END             ;EXIT IN SYNTAX TIME

                                              ;SYNTAX TIME
7D69 C3C105 DRAW#RUN JP    END1               ;TEMP RUN-TIME EXIT
                    END
```

Note that in syntax time a call to EXPT_1NUM only checks the syntax of an expression and does not evaluate it. Also, CH_ADD is advanced to the first code after the expression and the code is already in the A register.

Again the reader might like to confirm that the syntax module functions correctly before proceeding to consider the run-time module that follows.

The run-time module for **DRAW** n;

```
                ORG     7D69H              ;32105 DEC
7D69 D7         DRAW#RUN RST    CALBAS
7D6A 941E               DEFW    FND#INT1   ;N GOES INTO THE A REGISTER
                                           ;RANGE 0-255 ONLY
7D6C A7                 AND     A          ;TEST FOR N=0
7D6D 2005               JR      NZ,DRAW#R1 ;JUMP IF N IN RANGE 1-255
7D6F FD36000A           LD      (IY+ERR#NR),0AH ;BUT GIVE 'INTEGER OUT OF
7D73 EF                 RST     ROMERR     ;RANGE' IF N=0
                ;DEAL FIRST WITH OVER 1;
7D74 47         DRAW#R1 LD      B,A        ;SAVE THE VALUE N
7D75 3E15               LD      A,OVER     ;OVER CONTROL CODE
7D77 D7                 RST     CALBAS
7D78 1000               DEFW    PRINT#A1   ;PRINT OVER
7D7A 3E01               LD      A,01H
7D7C D7                 RST     CALBAS
7D7D 1000               DEFW    PRINT#A1   ;MAKE IT OVER 1;
                ;AND NOW N UNDERLINE CHARACTERS
7D7F 3E5F       DRAW#R2 LD      A,UNDLINE
7D81 D7                 RST     CALBAS
7D82 1000               DEFW    PRINT#A1   ;EACH UNDERLINE CHARACTER
7D84 10F9               DJNZ    DRAW#R2    ;IN TURN
7D86 C3C105             JP      END1       ;EXIT
```

Note that in run-time a call to EXPT_1NUM evaluates the numeric expression and places the result on the calculator stack; from where it is collected by FIND_INT1.

Also see how a 'main' error report is produced by loading the system variable ERR_NR with the appropriate value and exiting via Restart ROMERR.

CIRCLE n
The third new statement to be discussed allows the user to draw a circle of diameter 'n' around the current position.

In BASIC this might be mimiced by:
```
         10 LET X=PEEK 23677: LET Y=PEEK 23678
         20 CIRCLE X,Y,n        — user supplies n
         30 POKE 23677,X: POKE 23678,Y
```
But 'errors' occuring whilst in **CIRCLE** n will be trapped!

The syntax module:

The steps are:
- Fetch the command code and compare it to **CIRCLE**
- Look for a 'numeric expression'
  Call the ST_END routine

In assembly language this is:

```
                ; ADD THE FOLLOWING LINES TO THE "COMMAND SEARCH"
       FED8              CP      CIRCLE
       CA907D            JP      Z,CIRC#SYN    ;FOR CIRCLE N
                ;CIRCLE N - SYNTAX MODULE PROPER
                         ORG     7D90H         ;32144 DEC
7D90 D7         CIRC#SYN RST    CALBAS
7D91 2000                DEFW    NXT#CHAR      ;ADVANCE CH#ADD
7D93 D7                  RST     CALBAS
7D94 821C                DEFW    EXPT1NUM      ;FIND A NUMERIC EXPRESSION
7D96 CDB705              CALL    ST#END        ;EXIT IN SYNTAX TIME
```

The run-time module:

This module is to include 'error trapping' handling — i.e. any error that occurs will not result in the production of a report; instead the BASIC interpreter will proceed to the next statement.

The assembly listing for the module is:

```
                         ORG     7D99H         ;CIRCLE N RUN-TIME MODULE
                                               ;32153 DEC
7D99 2A7D5C     CIRC#RUN LD      HL,(COORDS)
7D9C E5                  PUSH    HL            ;COPY COORDS
7D9D 2A3D5C              LD      HL,(ERR#SP)
7DA0 E5                  PUSH    HL            ;COPY ERR#SP
7DA1 21CC7D              LD      HL,ER#ADD
7DA4 E5                  PUSH    HL
7DA5 ED733D5C            LD      (ERR#SP),SP   ;SET UP THE ERROR HANDLER
7DA9 D7                  RST     CALBAS
7DAA 941E                DEFW    FINDINT1      ;FETCH N
7DAC F5                  PUSH    AF            ;SAVE ON STACK
7DAD 3A7D5C              LD      A,(COORDS)    ;FETCH CURRENT X POSITION
7DB0 D7                  RST     CALBAS
7DB1 282D                DEFW    STACK#A       ;ON TO CALCULATOR STACK
7DB3 3A7E5C              LD      A,(COORDS+01H)
7DB6 D7                  RST     CALBAS
```

```
7DB7 282D          DEFW   STACK#A         ;SAME WITH Y POSITION
7DB9 F1            POP    AF              ;RETRIEVE N
7DBA D7            RST    CALBAS
7DBB 282D          DEFW   STACK#A         ;STACK IT ALSO
                   ;ON CALCULATOR STACK ARE X POSITION, Y POSITION
                   ;AND THE RADIUS N. THE CIRCLE CAN NOW BE DRAWN
7DBD D7            RST    CALBAS
7DBE 2D23          DEFW   CIRCLE#1        ;DRAW THE CIRCLE
7DC0 E1            POP    HL              ;DROP ERR#SP
7DC1 E1            POP    HL              ;RESTORE ERR#SP
7DC2 223D5C        LD     (ERR#SP),HL     ;CORRECTLY
7DC5 E1            POP    HL
7DC6 227D5C        LD     (COORDS),HL     ;RESTORE COORDS
7DC9 C3C105        JP     END1            ;EXIT IF SUCCESSFUL
                   ;OTHERWISE USE THE ERROR HANDLER
                   ;NOTE 'MAIN' ROM WILL BE IN USE
7DC7               ORG    7DC7H           ;32199 DEC
7DC7 E1    ER#ADD  POP    HL
7DC8 223D5C        LD     (ERR#SP),HL     ;RESTORE ORIGINAL ADDRESS
7DCB E1            POP    HL
7DCC 227D5C        LD     (COORDS),HL     ;RESTORE COORDS
7DCF FD3600FF      LD     (IY+ERR#NR),0FFH;NO ERROR AFTER ALL
7DD3 C9            RET                    ;EXIT WITH A RET ONLY AS
                                          ;'MAIN' ROM IN USE
```
Note the steps involved in 'trapping errors'.
Before:
- the current error address (ERR_SP) is saved
- a new error address is put on the machine stack
- ERR_SP is set to point to the address

After:
- the original address for ERR_SP is retrieved
- the 'error' is cancelled by setting ERR_NR to FFh.

BORDER *b,i,p
The fourth new statement to be discussed allows the user to change the TV display to:
        a **BORDER** colour 'b'
        an **INK** colour 'i'
        a **PAPER** colour 'p'
These colours will be 'permanent'. In addition the attribute bytes of the screen will hold the new **PAPER** colour. In BASIC this would be like:
        BORDER b: **INK** i: **PAPER** p: **CLS**
but the current picture will not be removed as with **CLS** and the 'current print position' will remain unaltered.

The syntax module:

The steps are:
- Fetch the command code and compare it to **BORDER**
- Confirm the presence of the separator '*'
- Look for three numeric expressions separated by commas
- Call the ST_END routine

In assembly language this is:

```
                ; ADD THE FOLLOWING LINES TO THE "COMMAND SEARCH"
     FEE7              CP       BORDER
     CAE07D            JP       Z,BORD#SYN        ;FOR BORDER B,I,P
                ;BORDER *B,I,P - SYNTAX MODULE PROPER
                       ORG      7DE0H             ;32224 DEC
7DE0 D7         BORD#SYN RST    CALBAS
7DE1 2000              DEFW     NXT#CHAR          ;ADVANCE CH#ADD
7DE3 FE2A              CP       '*'               ;IS THE SEPARATOR PRESENT?
7DE5 200A              JR       NZ,BORD#ERR       ;JUMP IF MISSING
7DE7 D7                RST      CALBAS
7DE8 2000              DEFW     NXT#CHAR          ;ADVANCE CH#ADD
7DEA D7                RST      CALBAS
7DEB 821C              DEFW     EXPT1NUM          ;THIS IS 'B'
7DED FE2C              CP       COMMA             ;LOOK FOR SEPARATOR
7DEF 2802              JR       Z,BORD#S1
7DF1 E7         BORD#ERR RST    SH#ERR
7DF2 00                DEFB     00H               ;'NONSENSE IN BASIC"
7DF3 D7         BORD#S1 RST     CALBAS
7DF4 2000              DEFW     NXT#CHAR          ;ADVANCE CH#ADD
7DF6 D7                RST      CALBAS
7DF7 821C              DEFW     EXPT1NUM          ;THIS IS 'I'
7DF9 FE2C              CP       COMMA             ;LOOK FOR SEPARATOR
7DFB 20F4              JR       NZ,BORD#ERR       ;BACK IF MISSING
7DFD D7                RST      CALBAS
7DFE 2000              DEFW     NXT#CHAR          ;ADVANCE CH#ADD
7E00 D7                RST      CALBAS
7E01 821C              DEFW     EXPT1NUM          ;THIS IS 'P'
7E03 CDB705            CALL     ST#END            ;EXIT IN SYNTAX TIME
                       END
```

Note how the three numeric expressions are fetched in turn by using EXPT_1NUM and that the separators between expressions must be 'commas'. BORD_ERR uses the Restart SH_ERR routine to signal an error that in run-time would be indicated by the error report 'Nonsense in BASIC'.

The run-time module:

```
                ORG      7E06H              ;32262 DEC
7E06 D7         BORD#RUN RST      CALBAS
7E07 941E                DEFW     FND#INT1   ;P GOES IN THE A REGISTER
7E09 FE08                CP       08H        ;ALLOW RANGE 0-7
7E0B 3005                JR       NC,BORD#R1
7E0D FD360013   BORD#K   LD       (IY+ERR#NR),13H ;'INVALID COLOUR'
7E11 EF                  RST      ROMERR
7E12 07         BORD#R1  RLCA                ;SHIFT ALONG THE BITS
7E13 07                  RLCA
7E14 07                  RLCA
7E15 5F                  LD       E,A        ;SAVE P#8 IN A REGISTER
7E16 D5                  PUSH     DE         ;AND ON MACHINE STACK
                ;NOW CHANGE ALL THE ATTRIBUTE BYTES
7E17 010003              LD       BC,0300H   ;THERE ARE '768' BYTES
7E1A 21FF57              LD       HL,57FFH   ;BASE ADDRESS-1
7E1D 23         BORD#R2  INC      HL
7E1E 7E                  LD       A,(HL)     ;FETCH EACH ATTRIBUTE
7E1F E6C3                AND      0C3H       ;AND ALTER THE PAPER
7E21 B3                  OR       E          ;BITS TO GIVE THE COLOUR
7E22 77                  LD       (HL),A     ;SPECIFIED BY P
7E23 0B                  DEC      BC
7E24 7B                  LD       A,B
7E25 B1                  OR       C
7E26 20F5                JR       NZ,BORD#R2 ;UNTIL ALL DONE
                ;CONSIDER THE NEW INK COLOUR
7E28 D7                  RST      CALBAS
7E29 941E                DEFW     FND#INT1   ;FETCH I
7E2B FE08                CP       08H
7E2D 30DE                JR       NC,BORD#K  ;REPORT K IF OUT OF RANGE
7E2F D1                  POP      DE         ;FETCH P#8
7E30 B3                  OR       E          ;ADD IN THE BITS
7E31 5F                  LD       E,A        ;RESULT TO E REGISTER
                ;CHANGE ATTR#P & ATTR#T
7E32 3A8D5C              LD       A,(ATTR#P) ;KEEP ANY FLASH AND
7E35 E6C0                AND      0C0H       ;BRIGHT BITS
7E37 B3                  OR       E          ;ADD IN I & P
```

```
7E3B 3280SC            LD      (ATTR#P),A      ;RESTORE THE VALUE IN
7E3B 328F5C            LD      (ATTR#T),A      ;BOTH LOCATIONS
                ;NOW CONSIDER B
7E3E D7                RST     CALBAS          ;THE BORDER COMMAND
7E3F 9422              DEFW    BORDER          ;ROUTINE CAN BE USED TO
                                               ;ADVANTAGE HERE
7E41 C3C105            JP      END1            ;FINISHED
                       END
```

Note that if the separator '*' is omitted from the syntax requirements of the **BORDER** *b,i,p statement then b can be left to be handled by the 'main' BASIC interpreter - but the syntax module must consider all parts of the statement even if a part is ignored by the run-time module.

CONCLUSION:

The four examples of 'new statements' for the **Spectrum** system are only meant to introduce the subject. It is hoped that the reader is now ready to try adding his/her own statements. Ideally the machine code programmer should have to hand copies of:

> 'Understanding Your Spectrum' by Dr Ian Logan
> 'The Complete Spectrum ROM Disassembly' by Dr Ian Logan & Dr Frank O'Hara
> 'BASIC programming' by Steven Vickers
> (the handbook for the ZX Spectrum)
> 'ZX Interface 1 & ZX Microdrive'
> (the handbook for these products)

and a good supply of time.

INDEX

B
baud rate 7, 63
BBC microcomputer 73
BORDER (new statement) 101
border colour 7, 42, 46, 65, 101
broadcast 45

C
CALBAS 7, 95
CAT 14, 23, 35
CH_ADD 95
channels — Microdrive 32
— Network 53
— RS232 70
CIRCLE (new statement) 99
CLEAR # 19
CLOSE # 27, 39, 49, 50
CLS # 18
CODE 16
COPIES 14

D
DATA 16
data file 22, 25
DRAW (new statement) 97

E
ERASE 14, 23, 35
error trapping 99

F
FORMAT 9, 22, 34, 45, 63

H
HEADER 53-61
hook codes 8, 77-91
— console input 78
— console output 79
— RS232 input 80
— RS232 output 80
— ZX printer output 81
— keyboard test 81
— select drive 81
— open file 82
— close file 82
— delete file 84
— read sequential 84
— write record 85
— read random 86
— read sector 86
— read next 86
— write sector 86
— create buffer 86
— delete buffer 89
— open network channel 89
— close network channel 89
— get packet 91
— send packet 91
— create system variables 91

I
INKEY$# 26, 39, 49, 58
INPUT # 26, 39, 49
insertion of shadow system
  variables 7, 91
IOBORD 7, 42, 46, 65
IRIS 43

L
LINE 16, 24
LINE (new statement) 96
LOAD 16, 24, 37, 46, 58
Local Area Network ..... see Network

M
Microdrive 21-42
— channel details 32
— technical details 28-42
— timing details 30
......
— cartridge 21
— **CAT** 14, 23, 35
— **CLOSE #** 27, 39
— connector 5
— **ERASE** 14, 23, 35
— **FORMAT** 9, 22, 34
— hook codes 81-89
— **INKEY$#** 26, 39
— **INPUT #** 26, 39
— **LOAD** 24, 37
— map (sector) 34, 37, 41
— **MERGE** 16, 24, 37
— **MOVE** 15, 27, 40
— named files 22, 30
— **OPEN #** 12, 26, 32, 38
— records 26, 40
— **SAVE** 23, 36
— sectors 22, 30, 34, 39-42
— tape format 30

— **VERIFY** 24, 37

N

Network 43-61
— channel details 32
— technical details 50-61
— timing details 59
.....
— broadcast 45
— **CLOSE #** 49, 50
— connector 5
— **FORMAT** 10, 45
— HEADER 53-61
— hook codes 89-91
— **INKEY$#** 49
— **INPUT #** 49
— LOAD 17, 46
— MERGE 18, 46
— NTSTAT 7, 45
— **OPEN #** 12, 46
— **PRINT #** 48
— SAVE 16, 45
— SCOUT 53-61
— **VERIFY** 18, 46
new statements 91-104
— **BORDER** 101
— **CIRCLE** 99
— **DRAW** 97
— **LINE** 96

O

OPEN # 11-13, 38, 48, 65

P

paging mechanism 6, 8
PRINT # 25, 40, 48
program files 22

R

RS232 link 63-75
— channel details 65
— technical details 70-72
— timing details 72
.....
— BBC microcomputer 73
— **CLOSE #** 66
— connector 5
— **FORMAT** 9, 64
— hook codes 80
— **INKEY$#** 66
— **INPUT #** 66

— LOAD 17, 64
— MERGE 18, 64
— **OPEN #** 13, 64
— **PRINT #** 66
— SAVE 17, 64
— T system 66
— **VERIFY** 18, 64
RS423 (BBC microcomputer) 73

S

SAVE 16, 36, 45, 64
SCOUT 53-61
SCREEN$ 17
SELF 43
shadow ROM 6, 7-13
Station 43
syntax/run-time modules 95

T

tape (**Microdrive**) 21
T system 90

V

VECTOR 94
VERIFY 18, 24, 37, 46, 64

Z

ZX Interface 1 5-8
ZX Printer 73

SPECTRUM MICRODRIVE BOOK

REGISTRATION CARD

Please fill out this page and return it promptly in order that we may keep you informed of new software and special offers that arise. Simply cut along the dotted line and return it to the correct address selected from those overleaf.

Where did you learn of this product?

☐ Magazine. If so, which one? ....

☐ Through a friend.

☐ Saw it in a Retail Store

☐ Other. Please specify ....

Which Magazines do you purchase?

Regularly: ....

Occassionally: ....

What age are you?

☐ 10-15   ☐ 16-19   ☐ 20-24   ☐ Over 25

We are continually writing new material and would appreciate receiving your comments on our product.

How would you rate this book?

☐ Excellent
☐ Good
☐ Poor

☐ Value for money
☐ Priced right
☐ Overpriced

Please tell us what software you would like to see produced for your SPECTRUM.

_____

_____

_____

Name _____

Address _____

_____ Code _____

PUT THIS IN A STAMPED ENVELOPE AND SEND TO:
In the United States of America return page to:
Melbourne House Software Inc., 347 Reedwood Drive, Nashville TN 37217.

In the United Kingdom return page to:
Melbourne House (Publishers) Ltd., Melbourne House, Church Yard, Tring, Hertfordshire, HP23 5LU

In Australia & New Zealand return page to:
Melbourne House (Australia) Pty. Ltd., Suite 4 Palmerston Crescent, South Melbourne, Victoria, 3205.